Albert Make Us Laugh

A play

Jimmie Chinn

Samuel French — London
New York - Toronto - Hollywood

ALBERT MAKE US LAUGH

Written for and first presented by The Questors Student Group at The Questors Theatre, Ealing on July 12th, 1986 with the following actors playing all the parts:

Gabriel Farrell, Stephen Hehir, Jane Allighan, Adrienne O'Brien, Kia Sian, Anne Kilborn, Paul Chinn and Denys Gaskill

Directed by the Author
Designed by Norman Barwick
Costumes by Brian Moorhouse
Lighting by Steve Hames and Miles Rendle

COPYRIGHT INFORMATION

(See also page ii)

ALBERT MAKE US LAUGH in its present form was first presented by Teddington Theatre Club at Hampton Court Theatre on October 24th, 1987 with the following cast:

Albert Nuttall	Peter Slater
Enid Nuttall	Merlyn Lowther
Headmaster Tope	Jack Smerdon
Miss Mint	Freda Hammerton
Miss Hemsley	Sue Viney
Miss Partington	Sue Scarrott
Mr Leatherbottle	Steve Taylor
Eric Smallshaw	Ken Mason
Primrose Macaveney	Patti Bottomley
Beryl Noten	Caroline Dooley
Shane Butterworth	Chris Hurles
Charlie Shorrocks	David Wheatley
Barbara Batch	Caroline Dabney
Lobelia Bottomley	Nancy Brown

Directed by the Author
Designed by Gordon Edwards
Lighting by Chris Davis and Mike Elgey
Costumes by Lynette Hatcher-Cushing and
    Sahra Lorimer-Gott
Sound by William Elliot

CHARACTERS

The Adults	The Children
Headmaster Tope	Albert Nuttall
Enid Nuttall	Primrose Macaveney
Miss Mint	A Little Girl
Miss Hemsley	Nora Tooley
Miss Partington	Barbara Batch
Mr Leatherbottle	Shane Butterworth
Eric Smallshaw	Charlie Shorrocks
	Lobelia Bottomley

DOUBLING

Miss Mint / A Little Girl
Miss Hemsley / Nora Tooley
Miss Partington / Barbara Batch
Mr Leatherbottle / Shane Butterworth
Eric Smallshaw / Charlie Shorrocks

NOTE: It is the nature of the play, and the intention of the author, that the children must be played by adult actors. The smallest number of players required is nine. If the Director does not wish to double then fourteen actors can be used with any number of extra (non-speaking) parts. Only Albert and Primrose, who are seen from the age of eleven to 21, and Headmaster Tope and Enid Nuttall are impossible to double.

Time — Ever so long ago. (Late 1940s — 1950s)

The action of the play takes place in and around Belmont Fields Secondary Modern School and in the home of Albert Nuttall

NOTES

To allow for a fluid and flexible production, staging is best done simply but imaginatively with maximum use of light and sound and music. Locations to be suggested: school playground, school hall, a classroom, sports hall, headmaster's study, Albert's home (with double bed) and several separate areas suggested by pools of light only. Costumes must suggest the late 1940s to 1950s.

To Albert — wherever he may be now
... and to Peter Slater whose sensitive and brilliant
performance brought him so vividly to life.
As ever,
J.C.

"A perfect childlike simplicity puts us at once
into intimate relationship with God,
without any hindrance."
From *Letters of Direction*
by the Abbé de Tourville

Other plays by Jimmie Chinn published by
Samuel French Ltd:

After September
But Yesterday
From Here To The Library
Home Before Dark, *or,* **The Saga of Miss Edie Hill**
In By The Half
In Room Five Hundred and Four
Interior Designs
Pity About Kitty
A Respectable Funeral
Something To Remember You By
Straight and Narrow
Take Away The Lady
Too Long An Autumn

ACT I

The play opens in darkness

Music: children singing "Jesus Loves the Little Children"

The Lights come up on the school hall; it is a sunny morning

The entire company (except for Enid and Headmaster Tope) enter dressed as eleven-year-old children, among them Barbara Batch, Shane Butterworth, Nora Tooley, Charlie Shorrocks and Lobelia Bottomley, the "boys" in short trousers, school caps, etc., the "girls" in frocks, white socks, hair ribbons, etc.

Albert himself is wheeled on in a push-chair by Enid, his mother

The scene takes the form of a parade with Albert as the centre-piece

Children (*singing loudly*) Vote, vote, vote for Albert Nuttall,
Vote for him because he's daft,
Albert is the one if you want a bit of fun,
But you'll all be sorry that you laughed!

They repeat the song once or twice and dance around Albert and Enid

Headmaster Tope enters and blows his whistle loudly

Everyone freezes

Tope speaks out loudly and clearly across the distance of Time and Space

Tope This is the story of little Albert Nuttall — who at the age of eleven arrived for his first day at Belmont Fields Secondary Modern School in a push-chair ...

Enid pushes Albert forward. Albert smiles disarmingly at all the attention he is being given. Enid, odd and alone as always, stares out into the middle distance

We knew at once that something was amiss.

All the children, one by one, introduce themselves to the audience with lines such as: "I'm Barbara Batch and I've forgotten my hanky", "I'm Shane Butterworth and I don't feel well," etc. etc. etc. Primrose is last

Primrose (*primly, a proper madam*) My name's Primrose Mary Macaveney and my mummy says I'm not to play with you because you are smelly and daft, and because you look up little girl's dresses to see their knickers, so there!

Albert smiles cheekily at us then lifts Primrose's dress from the back to reveal her navy blue knickers

(*Bursting into noisy tears*) You dirty, dirty beast!
Children (*singing*) Albert is the one if you want a bit of fun,
But don't tell your mother what he did!
Tope Every village has its idiot. Albert was ours. (*He blows his whistle again*)

The children form a line for morning assembly. Albert stands and moves to the middle

Enid stands aside with the empty push-chair, looking on but strangely invisible to the rest

(*Leading in to the hymn*) And one and two and …
Children (*singing*) All things bright and beautiful,
All creatures great and small,
All things wise and wonderful,
The Lord God made them all …

They sing one verse and another chorus of the hymn

Tope (*when the hymn is over, importantly*) Now, boys and girls, I want you to listen very carefully. I am Headmaster Tope … that is Tope … T.O.P.E..
Albert (*smiling*) Tope.
Tope And on behalf of the staff and all the other pupils of Belmont Fields Secondary Modern School I would like to welcome you on this, your very first day here. And when, in these morning assemblies, I say unto you "Good-morning, boys and girls of Belmont Fields", I shall expect you all to reply, in unison, "Good-morning, Headmaster". Now, is that clear? We'll have a little rehearsal, shall we? Good-morning, boys and girls of Belmont Fields.
Children Good-morning, Headmaster.

Tope Well done. Very nicely spoken. Now, you may all sit cross-legged on the floor.

All the children sit. Primrose has to pull at Albert's trousers to get him to sit. Enid remains, as if not there at all

Here at Belmont Fields we all start on the floor. In our second year we sit on the PT benches, in our third on the grown-up chairs, and in our fourth and final year we stand at the back of the hall with our feet slightly apart and our hands clasped modestly in front—like so. (*He demonstrates*) You, little boy, (*he points to Albert*) can you tell me why you think that is?

They all stare at Albert

Albert (*after a thought*) There aren't enough chairs, Sir.

His reply is not intended to be facetious or rude, it is simply common sense. Everyone laughs. Tope is obviously not amused. They all stop laughing

Tope I can see this pupil will excel at Maths. What is your name, little boy?
Albert (*shyly, too aware of the sudden attention*) Albert, Sir. Albert Nuttall.
Tope You will please stand.

Albert rises to his feet; the rest whisper to each other

(*Sternly*) Please!

There is silence

You will please not mutter, moan or merrymake when I am speaking. Is that understood? (*Louder*) Is it?
Children (*cowed*) Yes, Headmaster.
Tope (*to Albert*) Now, little boy. Tell this gathered multitude of fellow pupils your name.
Albert (*quietly*) Albert, Sir.
Tope Louder — lest we think we are going deaf.
Albert (*louder and with sudden pride*) I'm Albert, Albert Nuttall, and I live at number three, Paradise Mansions, Crabtree Common, and I live with my mum but not my dad because he's not there and never has been, and I went to Dorothy Street Juniors and now — I'm here ... Sir.
Tope (*lost for words*) You may be seated.
Albert Sir?

Tope Sit down.

Albert sits, helped by Primrose

I think we shall all remember this little boy's name — shall we not?
Children Yes, Headmaster.
Tope What is it?
Children Albert Nuttall, Headmaster.
Tope Correct. And we trust he will not turn out to be silly.

Primrose fidgets

You! Little girl. Stand.

Primrose stands

What is your *name*?
Primrose My name is Primrose Mary Macaveney, Sir.
Tope Tell me, Primrose Mary Macaveney, why do you fidget and fuss? Are
you wanting to be excused?
Primrose Please, Sir, Albert Nuttall is very smelly and has just made a
puddle on the floor, Sir.

Everyone gasps in horror

Tope Good gracious. In assembly. Whatever next. (*He points to Nora
Tooley*) You. Little girl. Stand up.

Nora Tooley stands

Name?
Nora Nora Tooley, Headmaster.
Tope Go at once, Nora Tooley, to the caretaker in his basement, and ask him
to fetch a bucket and mop forthwith.
Nora Yes, Sir. Can I take a friend, Sir?
Tope If you must, but go — quickly!

Nora exits with another little girl

(*To the others*) Well, don't sit in it. (*To Shane Butterworth*) You, boy,
name?
Shane (*standing*) Shane Butterworth, Headmaster.
Tope The whole of Shane Butterworth's row, stand and move two paces
backwards — now.

The children do as instructed. Albert remains where he is, now alone and still seated

It seems we shall need a boat to reach our first lesson.

Children (*singing like a chorus line*) Vote, vote, vote for Albert Nuttall,
    He's just peed upon the floor,
    We've had to stand aside,
    To avoid the ghastly tide,
    And we hope he doesn't do it any more!

They all sit again, cross-legged on the floor, just behind Albert

Tope Today, children, is a very special day. Can any one tell me why today is so special?

Children (*all, except Albert, with hands up*) Sir, Sir, Sir ——

Tope Yes ... the pretty little girl next to Shane Butterworth: begin by saying your name, child.

Barbara Batch, a girl with thick glasses and a squint, stands

Barbara Barbara Batch, Sir, and today is so very special, Sir, because it's my sister Angela's birthday, Sir, and she's in Form Four B and she's going to have a baby, Sir.

Tope (*covered in confusion*) Really? (*She calls out into the auditorium*) Mrs Marshall? Do we know about this? In my study later, please! (*To Barbara*) Thank you, Barbara Batch, you may be seated.

Barbara (*smugly*) Thank you, Sir. (*She sits again*)

Tope (*addressing the rest*) What I really meant, boys and girls, is that today is your first day at your new school — your first day here at Belmont Fields ——

Charlie Shorrocks puts his hand up

Yes, that little boy, what is it?

Charlie (*showing off*) This is our big school, Sir.

Tope It is indeed ... er ... name?

Charlie Charlie Shorrocks, Sir. My big brother was here, Sir. But he's in prison now.

Tope Ah — yes, well — send him our regards. Now, boys and girls, you are all eleven years old, an age when we must learn politeness and self-discipline, to wash our necks and our knees — and what else? Primrose Mary Macaveney?

Primrose (*showing off*) Clean our teeth, Sir.

Tope Very good, Primrose. One gold star will be placed by your name in the office of Mrs Marshall, our worthy school secretary.
Primrose Thank you, Sir.
Tope Can we think of anything else?

Many hands go up: "Sir, Sir, Sir"

Little Shane Butterworth?
Shane (*goodness glowing from within*) We mustn't play "Mothers and Fathers", Sir, because my mum says so.
Tope (*delighted by such purity*) Excellent, Shane Butterworth. And why mustn't we play "Mothers and Fathers"?
Shane Because it's nasty and naughty and not very nice and because it's very, very shocking and rude!
Tope Splendid. Mr Butterworth shall receive *two* gold stars and a House point because he's extremely far-seeing and religious.

They all freeze. The Lights on the school hall fade slightly and a pool of Light comes up DR

Miss Joyce Hemsley walks into the Light carrying Albert's file

Miss Hemsley (*to the audience*) Yes, I've known the child since he was five — well, longer, really, I suppose, we knew about him when he was born, illegitimately of course … Albert — he goes by the name of Albert Nuttall …

In the far distance, almost as an echo, we can hear children singing "Vote, vote, vote for Albert Nuttall"

The mother's called … (*She consults her file*)

A Light comes up on Enid

Enid (*calling out, almost a cry of anguish*) Enid.
Miss Hemsley (*unaware of Enid*) Enid. Actually, she calls herself Nuttall but we don't think that's her real name … She's a strange woman, seldom speaks, obviously retarded and not very clean I'm afraid; but it must be said she seems to take care of Albert — after a fashion. We haven't seen the house — two rooms actually — number three, Paradise Mansions, by the railway. I doubt if that's very clean either — but what can I be expected to do? (*She smiles at us*) Miss Hemsley, Joyce Hemsley, Health and Social Welfare, Division Three. (*She turns away, her face in shadow*)

Enid (*as if in answer to some question, speaking words she could only speak in a dream*) And it was warm ... warm ... with carpets ... red carpets ... and all the counters were full of beautiful things ... perfumes and glasses and silver ... and the smell of flowers hung in the air ... and the sound of voices ... talking, talking ... and I came to this counter with jewels ... pearls and big coloured beads ... and there was this pin ... shaped like a horse's head ... it was green and blue and gold ... and it shone ... with diamond eyes ... (*she begins to get distressed*) ... they led me to an office ... that had red carpet too ... a man ... two men ... big ... they emptied my bag all over the floor ... (*alone, frightened, crying*) ... and ... and ...

Miss Hemsley (*turning to Enid*) And the pin?

Enid (*bewildered*) The pin?

Miss Hemsley The pin with the horse's head?

Enid (*trying to avoid the memory*) Albert? I want Albert.

Miss Hemsley (*sharply*) You took it. Didn't you, Miss Nuttall? The pin. From the counter. You stole it.

Enid (*distressed, confused*) Enid. Albert.

Miss Hemsley (*speaking out to us*) The woman is also a thief!

The Lights quickly cross-fade back to the school hall

Miss Hemsley and Enid exit

Albert (*with his hand up*) Please, sir — can I have a golden star?

All the children laugh

Tope Did we all hear that, boys and girls? Albert Nuttall is demanding a golden star. (*He laughs*) Oh dear, oh dear, oh dear ... gold stars have to be earned here at Belmont Fields, we don't give them away willy-nilly; they have to be sought, worked for — and after your behaviour this morning I suspect it will be quite a while before you are in line for such an honour.

A handbell is rung loudly off

The morning bell has sounded and our working day has begun. You are soon to meet your form teachers — all of whom are very, very nice ... Day One of your new and exciting lives has begun: the trumpets are sounding, the call of the clarion, the beat of the drum!

Charlie (*under his breath*) He's friggin' mad!

Tope Let us pray.

All, except Albert, clap their hands together in prayer and close their eyes

Oh, Lord, hear this day our humble prayers. Grant, O Lord, that our days
at Belmont Fields be happy, full of sunshine and industry. May each day
be fruitful as we try to carry on Thy good work and at sunset may we come
happy and contented to our beds knowing that if you see fit to take us in the
night we might wake to look upon Thy glorious face and be blessed. In the
name of the Father, the Son ——

Albert (*smiling, eyes wide open*) — and the Holy Ghost.
Tope (*opening one eye*) Amen!
Children Amen.
Tope You will kindly stand.

The children stand

Lead on.

Tope exits with a flourish

The children exit, singing softly: "Vote, vote, vote for Albert Nuttall"

*Nearly all the Lights fade, leaving Albert, still cross-legged on the floor, in
his own pool of light*

Albert One potato, two potato, three potato, four ... five potato, six potato,
seven potato more ... (*He tries to count them on his fingers*) That's twenty-
eight potatoes altogether ... (*He smiles at us*) I'm not backward; I know
what backward means and I'm not. I understand everything they say. I can
spell "beautifulness" ... I can — I can spell it ... but I'm not going to. It
begins with a B; I know the rest but I'm not going to tell you. My mum is
beautifulness ... And Primrose Macaveney ... (*He lowers his voice*)
Charlie Shorrocks isn't, though. He weed on my shoe in the boys' toilets
because I saw him smoking and he said if I told anybody he'd wee on me.
But he did anyway. It isn't fair, is it?

*Charlie Shorrocks, wicked, with a Woodbine cupped in his hand, appears
behind Albert*

Charlie (*menacingly*) What's your name?
Albert (*terrified*) Albert.
Charlie Albert what? *Stinkbum?*
Albert Albert Nuttall.
Charlie Well, I'm going to call you Albert Stinkbum — got it?
Albert (*trying to smile*) Yeah.
Charlie Then say it.

Albert Albert Stinkbum.

Charlie I know your mum — everybody knows your mum — she's called Daft Enid, in't she?

Albert (*confused, upset*) My mum is my mum … is my mum.

Charlie You're bleedin' barmy. Your mum's a tart and a loony — in't she?

Albert (*close to tears*) No.

Charlie (*crouching down behind Albert, speaking over his shoulder*) She is. Now, what is she? A tart and a loony.

Albert I don't know what it means.

Charlie (*hurting Albert's neck*) Say it!

Albert I can spell "beautifulness" … B.U.T. …

Charlie Shut it and listen, Stinkbum ——

Tope (*calling from the darkness beyond*) Charles Shorrocks, in my office — at once — now!

Charlie I'm going to get you, Stinkarse. Playtime — right!

Charlie runs off into the darkness

Albert (*alone again, happy*) I do English — and Maths — and History and Geography — and Scripture — and … (*he thinks hard*) … PT — that's Physical Training — but I don't like it because it's very silly …

During the following, the classroom is formed behind him. The children each bring on a chair to put at their desk and sit in silence

And Woodwork. I'm making my mum a stool — to sit on — and Art … I'm making a thing with silver milk bottle tops to hang on our wall; it glitters at night when you shine a torch on it … (*He gets to his feet*) And when I grow up, when I'm a big man, I'm going to drive a bus or a train … (*his eyes aglow with excitement*) or a helicopter in the sky … (*He throws out his arms to become a helicopter*) That's beautifulness … !

Albert runs off making the noise of a helicopter

The Lights come up on the classroom. The children, still at their desks, are also impersonating helicopters with their arms

Albert's Light fades

The children start making a din — throwing paper, rubbers etc.

Miss Celia Mint, serene and elegant at all times, enters carrying books

The children, suddenly aware of her presence, fall silent one by one

Miss Mint (*after an effective pause*) I'm waiting for you to stand.

The children stand

Are manners a thing of the past? A bygone age? Another era? I shall have
to speak to the Headmaster about this. He'll be shocked. "Manners" is his
middle name. (*She pauses*) Good-morning, First Years.
Children (*in unison*) Good-morning, Miss ...
Miss Mint Mint. My name is Mint. I shall be teaching you English. As you
see, I carry books, which is a token of my station in life. So, you may all
say "Good-morning, Miss Mint".
Children Good-morning, Miss Mint.
Miss Mint Much better. You may sit.

The children sit

Have you had your speech of welcome from Mr Tope, our Head?
Children Yes, Miss Mint.
Miss Mint You may be surprised when I tell you that although I was not
present in the hall at the time, I know every word he uttered. I've heard it
all before, you see. What a kind man he is, our Headmaster, no?
Children No, Miss Mint.
Miss Mint Yes, Miss Mint.
Children Yes, Miss Mint.
Miss Mint He runs a tight ship here at Belmont Fields. I was offered a post
at a school superior to this but I refused it. "No," I said. "Although I have
to teach dunces and slackers and idlers, I shall remain loyal to Mr Tope."
(*She looks at the children*) I suppose you all say "somefink" and "ain't" and
put the "i" before the "e" in receive ... no?

No reply. The children all sit looking at Miss Mint, bewildered

English is the language of the gods; we shall speak it properly or not at all.

Albert arrives, late, making his helicopter noises

(*Staring at Albert*) Yes?

Albert smiles shyly and makes his way to an empty chair and sits

What have we here? A loon? Why are you late, young man?

Not understanding her heightened way of speaking, Albert just smiles

Has this child lost the power of speech or has he an affliction of the ears?
Barbara That's Albert, Miss.
Charlie He's a bit behind the door, Miss.
Miss Mint (*not familiar with this expression*) I'm sorry?
Charlie Only tenpence to the bob, Miss. Not all there.
Miss Mint (*delighted*) How splendid! A challenge, He'll be walking out of
here in four years' time quoting Shakespeare!

They freeze

The Lights cross-fade from the classroom to a pool of light DL

Tope and Enid walk into the light. Tope is holding Albert's school report

Tope You see, Mrs Nuttall, his reports are quite good — very good, some
of them. He's not a stupid boy, not a stupid boy at all; in fact, our Miss
Mint, Head of English, has very high hopes for him. Now that may
surprise you — hmm?

Enid just stares into space, lost

Yes, well, but we are rather worried about your son, Mrs Nuttall, and,
please, whatever you do, don't take what I have to say as a criticism,
but — well — we feel that he might take more care over personal
hygiene — washing and such. Shall we say he's a little careless over
cleanliness, hmm? Now, I'm sure you've had a word with him in
private, I know what these boys are like. (*He attempts a laugh*)
Enid (*very simply*) He's a good boy — he means no harm.
Tope (*genuinely moved by her simplicity*) I'm sure. May I suggest, Mrs
Nuttall, and please don't think for a moment that I wish to interfere, but we
could arrange a visit by our Miss Hemsley ——
Enid (*firmly*) No.
Tope She really might be able to help you, Mrs Nuttall.
Enid No. I love him. I see to him. He's my baby. He's all I've got, see?
Tope (*helpless*) Yes, I know ... and I'm sorry.

Enid and Tope walk away into the darkness

*The Light on Enid and Tope fades. The Lights come up again on the
classroom*

Miss Mint is reading to a spellbound audience of children

Miss Mint (*reading*) No mail — no post.
　　　　　　No news from any foreign coast,
　　　　　　No warmth, no cheerfulness, no healthful ease,
　　　　　　No comfortable feel in any member —
　　　　　　No shade, no shine, no butterflies, no bees,
　　　　　　No fruits, no flowers, no leaves, no birds,
　　　　　　November!

Silence. A little girl cries

Albert You read really smashing, Miss. It's beautifulness.
Miss Mint Thank you, Albert. You have a feel for poetry. I can always tell.
Charlie (*bored*) What's it all mean, Miss?
Miss Mint (*her smile disappearing*) I beg your pardon — did you speak?

Charlie mutters under his breath

　　Stand up, boy.

Charlie stands

　　On the chair.

Charlie stands on his chair, hands in pockets and embarrassed. The rest of the children giggle.

　　This is a pretty kettle of fish I must say. I've half a mind to report you to Mr Tope. But I know what would happen. Do you?

Charlie mutters to himself

　　Pardon?
Charlie No, Miss.
Miss Mint He'd have you. On the carpet. Toeing the line. He'd insist on a public apology. And take your hands out of your pockets, boy. (*She stares at him in fury*) Now, I shall try hard to forget this ever happened — sit down, you very silly boy.
Charlie (*under his breath as he sits*) You piggin' get!
Miss Mint (*not hearing this*) Now, First Years, our subject for today is "Dreams".
Children (*an echo*) Dreams …
Miss Mint That's it. Dreams. Now — no calling out — what are dreams?
Children (*all except Charlie*) Miss … Miss … Miss.

Miss Mint Yes, Barbara … you may answer.

Barbara Batch stands

Barbara (*overexcited, speaking very quickly*) Please, Miss, dreams is what
you dream at night, Miss, when you're tucked up in bed and fast asleep,
Miss, and you dream a dream and it's all nice and the sun is shining and the
grass is green and the sky is blue and in the morning you wake up and your
mummy says, "Did you dream?" and you did but you can't remember,
Miss. (*She sits, breathless but proud*)
Miss Mint That's very true, Barbara.

Charlie mutters again

Primrose Macaveney — tell us about your dreams.
Primrose (*standing*) I dream about when I'm a lady, Miss, a big lady, and
I shall be an actress and do tap and ballet and sing on the stage, and people
will give me flowers and I'll curtsy like this, Miss. (*She drops a deep
curtsy*) That's what I dream, Miss Mint.
Miss Mint (*enraptured*) You shall grow to be tall — like a willow, Primrose
Macaveney.
Primrose Yes, Miss Mint. (*She sits, flushed*)
Miss Mint (*to another girl*) Lobelia Bottomley.
Lobelia (*standing*) Please, Miss, I wouldn't like to sing and dance on the
stage like Primrose Macaveney. I would like to be a teacher like you, Miss.
And wear nice dresses and have nice hair like you, Miss. And read a poem
like you did, Miss.
Miss Mint Is that so, Lobelia?
Lobelia Yes, Miss.
Miss Mint Well, maybe you will, Lobelia. But I have to warn you: the life
of a teacher is very hard; a teacher has to be dedicated to her chosen
profession — she cannot fritter her time away on common pursuits as do
the hoi polloi. No dances, no going to the pictures, early to bed and early
to rise, church on Sundays. Do you think you're up to it, Lobelia?
Lobelia Oh, yes, Miss. (*She sits*)
Miss Mint Well, let us hope so. Shane Butterworth — what do you dream
about?
Shane (*standing*) I don't dream, Miss. It makes me bilious.
Miss Mint Oh, come now, Shane, everybody dreams. You mean you can't
remember them — is that it?
Shane Yes, Miss.
Miss Mint What about daydreams? Do you never dream about what will
become of you after Belmont Fields?

Shane When I'm a man, Miss?

Miss Mint Of course. Will you be a butcher? Or a cobbler? Will you drive a train or sit behind a desk in charge of important papers?

Shane I haven't thought, Miss. I've got asthma and my mum says I'm delicate by nature, Miss.

Miss Mint Oh, dear. Do you have a device which helps you to breathe?

Shane (*holding up his device*) Yes, Miss. And I mustn't do PT or Games, Miss, because my mum says so. I have a note.

Miss Mint Ahh, I see. You must present it to Mr Leatherbottle in the sports hall, but you must be prepared to be put through the mill. Mr Leatherbottle is one of nature's hearties and doesn't recognize asthma.

Shane turns pale and sits

Now, let us give out our new books upon which we shall write our name boldly, clearly and neatly ...

Albert (*happy at first*) I have nice dreams sometimes, Miss ... but most of the time I have just one — and it's horrible.

Miss Mint A nightmare, Albert?

Albert Yes, Miss ... a nightmare, Miss ... a nasty dream ... where I'm alone ... and it's cold ... and raining, Miss ... and there's a wind ... and I can't see my mum ... she's gone ... and I'm looking for her ... (*He starts to become distressed as he recounts the dream*) "Mummy," I call ... "Mummy" ... but she doesn't hear ... she's too far away ... and I'm standing at the corner of the street ... on a road ... and there are signposts but I can't read them ... the language is foreign and I can't read what they say, Miss ...

His voice starts to echo around the auditorium. During the following, a spot comes up on Albert and the classroom lights dim. Albert falls to his knees

The children exit quietly, taking their desks and chairs with them. A bench is set up for Albert and Shane to use later

And in the distance ... there's another road ... far, far in the distance ... and it's cold and raining ... and I can see my mum ... she's walking along that road and I call to her ... "Don't go that way," I cry out ... "It's the wrong way." (*He begins to cry*) But she doesn't hear me ... she doesn't even see me ... and then ... like magic ... the sun comes from behind the black cloud ... and it lights up the far distant road ... and I can see my mum ever so clearly now ... and I begin to float ... (*He becomes excited, reliving his dream*) Up and up I go ... higher and higher, Miss ... I can feel the wind in my face ... and the rain ... and I float on the air ... faster and faster — towards my mum until I'm right above her ... looking down on her ... and

Miss, I call out again ... "Mum — Mummy" ... and she stops, Miss ... she looks up to see who's calling ...

From the darkness beyond comes Enid, strange and lost. She stands just behind Albert

"I'm here," I call ... "I'm here" ... but she doesn't see me, Miss ... (*He cries, lonely, afraid*) She doesn't see me at all. (*He calls loudly*) "Mum — I'm here — I'm Albert — I'm Albert Nuttall!"

Enid doesn't see or hear

Please see me ... please, please see me ...

His fear seems to pass: the echo subsides and is gone

And then ... then ... (*his beaming smile returns*) I wake up, Miss ... and she's there ... by my side ... and she says, "Shh, Albert, shh" ... and she holds me tight ...

Enid holds him tight

And I know everything's all right, Miss. It's beautifulness ...

Mother and son hold each other tight

Music, strange and haunting, is heard at a distance

Miss Mint, alone in her own light, looks worried by what she has just heard

Miss Mint He sleeps with her. The boy, Albert, he sleeps with his mother. That surely can't be right — something must be done!

Black-out

From the darkness, the sounds of a noisy playground

The Lights come up on a playground

Albert is alone

Shane Butterworth enters with a flask and a box of sandwiches. He sits on a bench, lays out a napkin on his lap and starts to eat. Albert looks on in awe

Albert (*with his usual disarming smile*) Hallo.

Shane I wish you wouldn't watch me eat. I don't like it.

Albert (*not understanding*) Yeah.

Shane Don't you have school dinners either?

Albert No.

Shane Then where are your sandwiches?

Albert I haven't got any.

Shane You mean you don't eat? Don't you like school dinners?

Albert I've never had them.

Shane Neither have I — but my mum says they're not very nice. I can only eat certain kinds of food because of my stomach. I have soup and freshly cut sandwiches. Would you like one?

Albert (*eyes aglow*) Yeah.

Albert sits beside Shane. They eat

Shane You could have some soup but I'm not allowed to share my cup, see. I might catch something. Are you backward?

Albert I think so.

Shane You should be in a special school, a school for backward people; there's one in Albatross Street.

Albert I wouldn't like it. I like it here.

Shane It's all right but my mum wanted me to go to grammar school but I failed my Eleven-plus, but not because I'm backward like you, it's because I missed so many lessons with my asthma. Have another sandwich. I'll bring more tomorrow. You should eat, you know, otherwise you waste away and die. What about your mum and dad: don't they feed you?

Albert My mum gives me beans on toast and chocolate biscuits. I haven't got a dad.

Shane What never?

Albert Never.

Shane I'm sure you must have had one once. It's something to do with nature.

Primrose Macaveney and Barbara Batch enter behind Shane and Albert. They have a skipping rope with them

Primrose (*peevishly*) That's not fair, Barbara Batch — you said if I gave you two of my barley sugars I could have a go with your rope.

Barbara I did not — so there.

The girls sulk in silence; during the following they then take turns to use the skipping rope

Shane (*to Albert*) There's Primrose Macaveney and Barbara Batch. They're

very silly. Don't look at them, Albert, they only want to spoil everything. Girls do that. My mum says I'm to have nothing to do with girls: they spread diseases. And you know you must never kiss a girl, don't you?
Albert I never have. I kiss my mum, though.
Shane That's different. But if you kiss a girl she starts to have a baby and then you have to get married to her and they take all your sandwiches!

Albert stares at the girls

Don't look at them — they might want us to kiss them.
Primrose (*seeing Albert staring at her:to him*) Got your eyeful, have you? What are you staring at?
Albert (*bashful*) Nuffink.

The girls giggle together

Shane (*putting his sandwiches away*) I told you not to look at them — that's how it all starts. Will you be my friend?
Albert (*in awe*) Yeah!
Shane Right. You can't be my very best friend because Neville Smallpiece is my very best friend but he goes to grammar school because he didn't have to miss lessons — but you can be my best friend here if you like. (*Rising*) Think about it anyway — I'll give you till tomorrow. Is tomorrow Tuesday?
Albert I don't know.
Shane I think so. Well, it'll be cheese tomorrow; it's always cheese on Tuesdays. I have to go and open my bowels now. You should always open your bowels after you've eaten, or you die.

Shane exits, not looking at the girls

The girls continue to giggle and whisper about Albert. After a while, Barbara comes and sits near Albert. Primrose performs a tap or ballet dance to show off

Barbara Hallo, Albert.
Albert (*still watching Primrose*) Hallo.
Barbara You know my friend? Primrose Macaveney?
Albert Yeah.
Barbara Do you think she's attractive? Nice looking?
Albert (*shy*) Yeah.
Barbara Do you want to go with her?
Albert (*not understanding this sophisticated talk*) Where to?

Barbara Well, she says that if you want to kiss her you can't, see, because she can't bear you near her because you smell all the time. Don't you ever have a bath?

Albert We haven't got a bath.

Barbara You could go to the public baths — you can go for nothing if you're very, very poor. Is your Mummy sick?

Albert No.

Barbara Sick in the head I mean ...

Charlie Shorrocks enters the playground, holding a Woodbine: there is immediate tension. Primrose stops dancing and Barbara moves back to join her. Albert cowers on the bench

Charlie Got a light, Stinkbum?

Albert No.

Charlie Mister!

Albert No, mister.

Charlie Oh, yeah, I forgot; you're a goody-goody. You don't smoke, you just stink.

Albert No.

Charlie (*grabbing the back of Albert's neck*) What?

Albert (*in pain*) Yes.

Charlie That's better. These your girlfriends then? Primrose Macaveney and Barbara Batch — eh?

Albert No.

Charlie (*grabbing Albert again*) What? What did you say, Stinkarse?

Primrose (*showing her true colours*) Leave him!

Charlie Shut it, Macaveney!

Primrose (*coming boldly forward*) I said leave him — and stop calling him rude names.

Barbara (*terrified*) Primrose — don't!

Charlie (*still holding on to Albert*) Oh, yeah — and what will you do about it, eh?

Primrose I shall report you to Miss Mint and she'll tell the Headmaster — so there. Now, take your hands off him.

Charlie Frig off, Macaveney.

Primrose (*hands on hips*) I'm warning you, Charlie Shorrocks. (*She grabs the skipping rope from Barbara*)

Charlie Get stuffed.

Primrose Right, Shorrocks, you've asked for it!

Primrose throws the rope over Charlie's head so that his arms are pinned to his side

Quick, Barbara, get him. Kick him.

The girls attack Charlie

Charlie (*helpless under the attack*) You little sods …

Albert is now laughing, enjoying all this

Primrose That's it, Barbara — kick him — kick him in the willy — the willy — go on.

Barbara, horrified, closes her eyes and kicks Charlie in the crotch: he doubles up in agony

Primrose and Barbara run off screaming and laughing

Albert hasn't the sense to run away too. Charlie gets to his feet and grabs Albert

Charlie I'm going to get you, Stinkarse … I'm going to piggin' get you for this!

Charlie punches Albert in the stomach and runs off

Albert is left winded and crying

Music fills the auditorium

The Lights fade on the playground leaving a warm pool of light on Albert

Enid, sad, lonely and untidy, appears from the darkness. She sits beside Albert who looks up at her and smiles: all is well now she's here. She offers Albert a bar of chocolate which he leans forward and bites into like an animal. They hold each other with great affection

The Lights come up and the scene becomes the Headmaster's study. The music fades

Tope and Miss Hemsley enter and become part of the scene

Tope We feel your son is not properly cared for, Mrs Nuttall. Now, please — we realize only too well how you are situated.
Albert My mum does care for me, Sir.

Miss Hemsley (*kindly*) We're quite sure she does, Albert. That's not what the Headmaster means, but — well, for instance, you've never had a holiday have you? You've never been to the seaside?
Albert No.
Miss Hemsley And you'd like to go to the seaside, wouldn't you?
Albert Would Mummy Enid come?
Miss Hemsley Well, I'm sure that can be arranged. What would you say to that, Enid?

No reply. Silence

Tope Mrs Nuttall — it would help if you'd just talk to us. How can we be expected to help if you remain silent?
Albert (*taking Enid's hand*) Mummy?
Enid (*to Albert*) Tell them we don't need help.
Albert She says ...
Tope (*with slight impatience*) I'm sorry, Mrs Nuttall, but we think you do need help and it would be wrong of us to stand by and do nothing. Albert's a growing boy; he's nearly thirteen and look at him. He's dirty and he smells, he has head lice and sores on his body. Now, either you allow Miss Hemsley to come and inspect your living quarters or she will have to inform the authorities who will have no choice but to force their way into your home!

Silence

(*Sorry he lost his temper: quietly*) I'm sorry.
Albert (*to Enid, gently*) Wouldn't you like to go to the seaside?
Enid (*looking at Miss Hemsley for support*) He doesn't understand. He's backward.
Tope (*sincerely*) But that's just it — he's not at all backward, Mrs Nuttall. He's intelligent and good at his lessons. Albert — spell beautifulness.
Albert (*proudly*) B.E.A.U.T.I.F.U.L.N.E.S.
Tope And?
Albert S. (*He smiles*)
Tope Good boy. You see, our Miss Mint has worked wonders with him. She's very proud of Albert.

Silence. Dead end: no one knows what to say next

Miss Hemsley Perhaps I could have a word with Enid alone.
Tope Enid?
Miss Hemsley She prefers to be called Enid. Perhaps you could take Albert to his next lesson, Headmaster.

Tope Very well. What is your next lesson, Albert?

Albert PT with Mr Leatherbottle, Sir.

Tope (*wincing*) Oh, God! Come along then — I'd better come with you. Into the lions' den, eh?

Albert I don't like Mr Leatherbottle, Sir.

Tope Nobody likes Mr Leatherbottle, Albert, but it's a cross we all have to bear. Have you got your PT kit?

Albert I haven't got any, Sir. My mum can't afford it, Sir.

Tope (*to Miss Hemsley*) Life is never easy.

Albert is led away by Tope

Enid makes to follow them

Miss Hemsley Enid — if I talk will you listen? Please?

Enid turns her head away in silence

I know you don't like me, or at least you don't like what I stand for, but I'm only here to help. We could provide you with a new home, Enid. A bigger place — with a bathroom and an inside toilet.

There is a pause: Enid does not answer

We're not going to take Albert away from you — we're not going to do that, Enid.

There is a long pause

Have you always lived in these two rooms? Have you?

Enid (*quietly*) Yes.

Miss Hemsley (*relieved to have an answer*) With your mother and father?

Enid Yes. And — and — him.

Miss Hemsley Him?

Enid My brother.

Miss Hemsley What happened to your parents, Enid?

Enid (*slowly*) They — they went away — away to ...

Miss Hemsley (*kindly but firm*) You mean they died, Enid. They died.

Enid Yes.

Miss Hemsley They died when you were quite young did they?

Enid Yes. When I was ... twelve.

Miss Hemsley And who took care of you then? Your brother?

Enid Yes. He — he was good to me ... he loved me. (*She looks up at Miss Hemsley for the first time*)

Miss Hemsley (*taking Enid's hand*) I'm sure he did, Enid. I'm sure he did. (*Gently*) What was his name?

No reply. Enid looks away

Where is your brother now? Where is your brother now, Enid?

Deep within, Enid longs for a friend, someone she can trust, but as yet the time is not right. She cries softly. Overcome by pity for this poor woman, Miss Hemsley takes her in her arms

The Lights fade to Black-out

The sounds of a noisy sports hall fill the darkness

A whistle blows loudly as the Lights come up on the sports hall. Standing there, in his PT gear, is the dreaded Mr Leonard Leatherbottle. His "class" is out in the auditorium

Leatherbottle (*shouting, of course*) No, no, no, no, you stupid boy! What the hell are you supposed to be doing? You're expected to jump *over* the horse — not kill your ruddy self by running into it! (*His eyes to heaven*) God in heaven, what have they sent me? Charlie Shorrocks, take your hands out of your shorts and stop playing with yourself, Now, come on, take a long run at it — run, lad, run — now JUMP! (*Horror registers on his face*) I can't stand it. Shorrocks. What are you? A sodding cripple or what? What? (*He cups his ear for the reply*) Sir, if you don't mind; I'm called "Sir" — not "cock", cock!

Tope and Albert enter rather sheepishly at the back

What was that, Shorrocks? Was that filth you came out with? Get to that changing room, wash those stinking feet and wait in my office. I'll give you "bollocks" — whatever they are!

Tope winces

(*Turning to see Tope; with great sarcasm*) Ah, children of Belmont Fields, we have company — we have honoured guests in the sports hall. Look who's popped in to see us — our Headmaster and young Nuttall.
Tope (*putting on a brave face*) May we have a word, please, Mr Leatherbottle? So sorry to interrupt the sterling work.

Tope whispers in Leatherbottle's ear then hurries away

(As he goes) Carry on, boys and girls, carry on.

He exits

Leatherbottle blows his whistle loud and long. The lesson stops. Silence. Leatherbottle points to the floor and Albert rushes forward and sits, cross-legged. Albert smiles disarmingly throughout the following onslaught

Leatherbottle Now, Second Years — I want you to take a look at this boy. This boy is Nuttall — Nuttall, children — and not only is he a sight for sore eyes — dirty, scruffy, filthy — but he's also a little creep; he brings notes from his mother, notes which are mis-spelt and as grubby as he is, notes which proclaim that he doesn't want to do PT with yours truly ... *(Shouting)* Gawshaw — are you listening? And today he crawls in here with the Headmaster, no less, who informs yours truly that Albert creep, creep Nuttall cannot do PT because he hasn't brought his togs. Now, children, I require your help: I want to know if at any time during the last two years you have seen Albert Nuttall in his PT togs. Because I haven't. Am I being unfair, I ask myself? Am I going blind? Do I need a white stick? Am I wrong in thinking all this is just eyewash? *(He pauses)* Hands up any boy or girl in this sports hall who has seen — ever — Albert Nuttall in his togs. *(He awaits a reply)* What — not a hand? Not one single hand?

Charlie Shorrocks, unseen by his teacher, enters behind Leatherbottle: he is dressed only in a pair of baggy black shorts. He starts silently to impersonate the PT master. The other children laugh

Is there no one here who will support poor little Albert Nuttall? *(Angry)* The Macaveney girl! Why are you laughing?

Albert is trying hard not to laugh at Charlie's antics. Charlie impersonates Hitler during the following

Now, hear this: I will not tolerate grubby little, stupid little, dirty little boys who do not want to do Physical Training twice a week, two hours a week, twenty hours a term, sixty hours a year, or my name's not Leatherbottle! Right?

Charlie suddenly turns his back, drops his shorts, and shows his bum

Black-out

Music fills the theatre

Albert goes over and joins Enid for the next scene

The music fades. There is the sound of a train rushing past

The Lights come up on a squalid room with a double bed; this is Albert's home. It is evening. Enid is on the bed playing with her rag dolls and talking to them. Albert is washing his face in a bowl of water

Another train rushes by outside

Albert (*after a while*) I've finished, Mum. See. Shiny face.
Enid Good boy, Albert. (*She screws up her face*) I'm ready.

Albert starts to wash Enid's hands and face with a cloth

We have to keep ourselves very clean, Albert.
Albert (*making the washing into a game as if dealing with a child*) One little hand. Two little hands.
Enid "Clean and tidy — spick and span ..."
Albert "Send away the bogey man!"

They both laugh: two children

I had a shower at school. It was nice. Hot and splashing. Like rain.
Enid We like rain.
Albert Do I smell nice?
Enid (*smelling him*) Yes. Of soap.
Albert Carbolic. That's what it's called. Carbolic soap. And coal-tar shampoo in my hair. Miss Hemsley gave it to me.
Enid (*the very name making her suspicious*) Where?
Albert At the hot shower. She gave me carbolic soap and coal-tar shampoo. And she dressed me in underpants — see.
Enid (*jealous*) I could have got them for you.
Albert That's what I told Miss Hemsley — but she said it would save you money. (*Excited, he produces a pair of pyjamas from somewhere*) And see ... (*He holds the pyjamas up*)
Enid (*warily*) What is it?
Albert (*proudly*) Jammas. Miss Hemsley said they're called jammas and I'm to wear them to bed instead of my school shirt.
Enid (*childishly*) Don't like them, Albert.

Obviously upset by her attitude, he folds away the pyjamas and offers Enid a mug of tea. Sulking now, Enid refuses it. Albert drinks his own tea in silence

Does she ask you questions? Miss Hemsley.

Albert Sometimes. Can I have a chocolate biscuit?

Enid You'll have none for the morning.

Albert (*counting the biscuits in the tin*) I've got four. I can have two now and two in the morning. Two and two is four — see. (*He eats*)

Silence: something unspoken hangs in the air

Enid (*at length*) Miss Hemsley. What sort of questions does she ask?

Albert All sorts. But I needn't answer if I don't want. She always says that.

Enid Does she ask about our house?

Albert Sometimes.

Enid Tell her nothing, Albert. Tell her to mind her own business. (*Pause*) They want to split us up, Albert. They want to send you away.

Albert (*not understanding*) What?

Enid They say I'm not good enough for you.

Albert Why would they do that? We're fine. We're happy. Aren't we?

Enid (*holding him to her*) Yes ... we are.

Albert (*after a while, not wanting to ask it*) Will you have to go to prison, Mummy?

Enid (*releasing him, angry*) Who said that? Who said it? (*Shaking him*) Who said it, Albert?

Albert Miss Hemsley said you did a bad thing — you went into a big shop and you stole things ...

Enid I did not — you mustn't believe them — I was ill — I didn't know what I was doing.

Albert (*relieved*) So you won't go to prison? (*He smiles*) I knew you wouldn't — I knew if I prayed they wouldn't send you away. Miss Partington says you have to pray to the Lord Jesus, every night before you go to sleep: you have to kneel down, see ... (*he kneels by the bed*) — and you have to say, "Dear Lord Jesus, just before I go to sleep, I pray you, Lord, my soul to keep, and if I should die before I wake, I pray you Lord my soul to take ..."

Enid It's all rubbish, Albert. There's no Lord Jesus. No Lord, no Jesus, no nothing. I did that once, I knelt down and prayed, but nothing happened. Nothing at all.

Silence. The Lights grow dimmer. A train rushes by outside

Albert's face lights up: he remembers something and rushes over to a chest of drawers and brings out a brown paper parcel

Enid (*child-like*) What's that?

Albert (*excited*) A present.
Enid (*eyes aglow*) A present? For you?
Albert No. For Mummy Enid. You.

Enid grabs the parcel and tears it open in her excitement: inside are a bar of soap, a bottle of dark brown shampoo, and a nightdress, secondhand but clean and ironed

Enid (*disappointed*) What are they?
Albert Miss Hemsley sent them. See, carbolic soap, coal-tar shampoo —
   and jammas.

Enid, wary at first of the nightdress, holds it up against herself as if it were a ballgown in a fairy story

Miss Hemsley says it's only one of her old ones but it's very nice and clean.
(*With wonder in his voice*) Do you like it?

Enid is thrilled; her face is full of wonder as she holds the nightdress up against herself

The Lights fade as the room set is struck

From the darkness we hear a children's choir singing "Silent Night"

A ring of bright Light comes up DR

Miss Janet Partington walks into the light

Miss Partington (*reading from a Bible*) "And Mary answered, 'My soul
   tells me of the greatness of God, and my spirit thrills in God my Saviour,
   because he has looked kindly on his servant though my place in life is
   humble — from now and for all time to come I shall be called blessed …'"
   (*She looks up*)

The pool of Light melts into an area of Light to represent Miss Partington's classroom

(*Angry, tired, strained*) Charles Shorrocks! Marigold Tucker! What are
you doing? (*She closes her book*) Why, oh why, do I bother? I'm reading
you the greatest story ever told and all you can do is pass obscene notes
around the class.

Albert, looking very upset, enters the area of light

(*Taking her anger out on Albert*) Albert! Why are you late? The lesson is nearly over.

Albert (*weeping softly*) I was kept in, Miss Partington.

Miss Partington By whom?

Albert Mr Ram, Miss.

Miss Partington (*gentler now*) Albert, you are mumbling and I cannot hear you. Mr Ram did you say?

Albert Yes, Miss.

Miss Partington (*seeing his distress*) Oh, dear ...

A handbell sounds loudly, off

(*Addressing her class*) The rest of you may go to your next lesson. Happy Christmas to you all ... (*She awaits a reply*)

Obviously no answer comes. Miss Partington looks sad and unhappy — a young woman, very pretty, who knows no joy

Come along, Albert. We'll sit down together and you can tell me all about it. (*They sit*) Now, tell me, why do you cry? It's Christmas — we mustn't cry at Christmas. What happened that Mr Ram kept you from my lesson?

Albert Please, Miss Partington, I made a noise, Miss, but I couldn't help it, Miss.

Miss Partington And why did you make a noise, Albert? You know Mr Ram hates noise in his classes.

Albert I couldn't help it, Miss. It's nature, isn't it?

Miss Partington What's nature?

Albert Making a fart, Miss.

Miss Partington Oh, I see. That kind of nature.

Albert Yes, Miss — and they all laughed at me and Mr Ram kept me in and I had to miss your lesson. It isn't fair, Miss, is it?

Miss Partington No, Albert. But life isn't always fair, I'm afraid.

Albert Not even at Christmas?

Miss Partington Oh, even less at Christmas sometimes.

Albert I've been praying — like you said, Miss. But it doesn't seem to make a lot of difference. I haven't seen Him yet.

Miss Partington Seen who?

Albert The Lord, Miss.

Miss Partington Oh, I see. Well, I'm sure you will see him — eventually.

Albert But when? I want him to help my mum get better.

Miss Partington Your mum. Why — is she ill?

Albert She coughs — and makes noises when she breathes, Miss ... and in the night when she's fast asleep.

Miss Partington Oh, dear, I am sorry. Have you seen a doctor about her?
Albert No, Miss.
Miss Partington (*becoming concerned now*) Look, Albert: your mother needs to see a doctor soon.
Albert Where?
Miss Partington At home. He'll come to your house with his bag and a thermometer and he'll prescribe some medicine for her.
Albert (*liking the word*) Prescribe.
Miss Partington That's what doctors do.
Albert But she won't let anybody in, Miss. She's frightened of Miss Hemsley; she says Miss Hemsley's got a big lorry and she'll take me away to the seaside and I won't come back again, Miss.
Miss Partington (*overwhelmed, taking his hand*) Oh, Albert, that's silly.

He quickly takes his hand away

I'm sorry, I thought you and I were friends?
Albert My mum says I'm not to have any friends: they might be spies of Miss Hemsley.
Miss Partington (*very worried now*) Albert — what are you and your mother doing at Christmas?
Albert What do you mean, Miss?
Miss Partington Well ... are you seeing friends, having a party?

Obviously he doesn't understand this

Albert: does your mum buy you a present at Christmas?

He hangs his head

(*Rising*) Albert, I'm going to see the Headmaster. You go to your next lesson. (*She turns to go*)
Albert Shall I keep on saying my prayers, Miss?
Miss Partington (*stopping*) Well ... (*She turns to him*) No, Albert, no. I fear it's a waste of time.

The Lights fade

As they do so, Miss Partington walks away

Music: children singing another Christmas song (perhaps "Little Donkey")

Bright Lights — like stage lights — come up on the school hall setting

Primrose Macaveney, wearing a long blue dress with an enormous cushion stuffed up it, and Shane Butterworth are rehearsing the parts of Mary and Joseph for the Nativity play under the expert direction of Miss Mint. A large wicker property basket stands nearby

Shane (*bored and very unnaturally*) Oh, Mary, Mary, I am so weak and weary ... we shall have to find an inn in which we can spend the long, lonely night. Oh dear, oh dear, oh dear ...

Miss Mint (*having seen enough*) No, no, no, no, no! Shane Butterworth — have you no soul? These are wonderful lines. You must speak them with imagination, with dignity!

Shane I don't want to be an actor, Miss. My mum says all actors are Jessies.

Miss Mint (*outraged*) Jessies! Your mother needs her hands and face smacked by the sound of it. Sir Donald? Sir Laurence? Jessies?

Shane The lines don't sound real, Miss, and I can't remember them.

Miss Mint I beg your pardon, this happens to be my play — I wrote these lines. We have done this play here at Belmont Fields for the last ten years and Mr Tope cries every time. Now, let's get to the inn — where's Charlie Shorrocks? He's supposed to be the innkeeper.

Primrose He'll be having a sly fag, Miss.

Miss Mint That boy will be dead before he's seventeen. All right, Shane, just get on with it.

Shane (*in character again*) We need a room for the night, Good Innkeeper; my good lady, Mary is heavy with child and will give birth this night.

Primrose begins to make moaning sounds

Miss Mint (*staring at her*) Primrose, dear — what are you doing?

Primrose I'm making pregnant noises, Miss. That's what they do. I asked Betty Bickerstaff in Four C and she said ...

Miss Mint Try to keep it subtle, dear.

Shane (*worried*) We're not having a real donkey are we, Miss? Only with my asthma I can't act with animals.

The handbell is sounded, off

(*Quickly removing his costume*) That's it. Time for my tablet, Miss.

Miss Mint Tablet?

Shane If I don't take my tablet it'll bring on my asthma. See you tomorrow, Miss.

He exits

Miss Mint (*sitting, exhausted*) That boy's a walking disaster. He's going to die during the performance and embarrass us all.

Primrose Have we finished, Miss?

Miss Mint It looks like it, Primrose.

Primrose (*sitting beside Miss Mint*) Please, Miss, my mum thinks I should do my tap number—in the second half, Miss, after I've had the baby, Miss.

Miss Mint Primrose, this is a religious piece, a nativity play — not *The Desert Song!*

Primrose My dad wants me to sing and dance, Miss.

Miss Mint Now, run along, dear: nine-thirty sharp in the morning, remember.

Primrose Can we miss Geography, Miss? Only Mr Ram doesn't like us being in plays, Miss.

Miss Mint The Philistines are upon us, Primrose. Leave Mr Ram to me — I know enough about Mr Ram and his nature rambles to have him put inside!

Primrose (*puzzled*) What, Miss?

Miss Mint Cut along, dear. And Primrose ...

Primrose Yes, Miss?

Miss Mint Couldn't you find a smaller cushion?

Primrose (*disappointed*) Yes, Miss.

As Primrose exits, Janet Partington enters the hall

Miss Mint starts to pack props and other items into the basket

Miss Mint Janet, dear.

Miss Partington Have you finished?

Miss Mint Just about. Are you all right?

Miss Partington (*sitting*) Do you ever wonder what it's all for?

Miss Mint Life? Or Teaching?

Miss Partington In our case they're both the same, aren't they?

Miss Mint Oh, dear. You are depressed.

Miss Partington Religious Education is the wrong subject for me, Celia.

Miss Mint (*producing an apple and beginning to eat it*) Wrong subject for anyone, dear. Never mind, soon be the Christmas hols — two weeks away from this place.

Miss Hemsley enters cheerfully

Hemsley Cooee, girls. What's this: no staff room, no Xmas lunch?

Miss Mint Janet's down in the dumps, Joyce.

Miss Hemsley Oh, dear; beginning to question your motives, are you, Janet? Fatal, lovey.

Miss Partington What are we going to do about Albert Nuttall? We can't sit by and do nothing, can we?

Miss Hemsley Don't insult me, Janet, please. I do all I can — so does the Head.

Miss Partington I'm sorry, Joyce — I didn't mean to sound ...

Headmaster Tope enters carrying his lunch on a tray

Tope Ah, ladies, I thought I heard voices. A quiet corner. I'm not disturbing you?

Miss Partington We have to do something about Albert Nuttall, Headmaster. We go on day after day and we do nothing at all!

Miss Mint Really, Janet!

Miss Hemsley The mother has a court case next month, for shoplifting. We're hoping she'll be put away; then we can get into the house, see the state it's in and get Albert put into care.

Miss Partington But that's ridiculous, Joyce. He couldn't manage without his mother — nor she without him.

Tope Miss Partington — please — the children might hear.

Miss Partington I don't care who hears, Mr Tope. Something's got to be done for that boy and his mother and it's got to be done now!

Silence. Miss Partington is obviously very upset. The others look on, helpless

(*Calmer now*) Look, I don't achieve much in this God-forsaken academy of learning. I try to teach religion to heathens and agnostics — and for what?

Tope Miss Partington, I think you should go and lie down.

Miss Partington I don't want to lie down. And please stop looking embarrassed, Headmaster; I can cope with that less than my failure as a teacher.

Miss Hemsley You're not a failure, Janet; don't be silly.

Miss Partington By what yardstick can you judge, Joyce? You're not even a teacher.

Miss Hemsley (*getting heated now*) I am a social worker, Janet. I, too, know what it feels like to be a failure. Have you any idea what it's like to arrive at a house, to offer help with problems I don't know the first thing about, and to be told to —— ?

Tope Ladies, please!

Miss Hemsley (*crying now*) I'm sorry, Headmaster, but I can get just as impassioned as Janet Partington. (*She wipes her tears with her handkerchief*) I'm so sorry.

Miss Mint, also upset, puts an arm around Miss Hemsley's shoulder

Miss Mint Really, Janet, Joyce is very, very upset.
Miss Partington In the name of God, Celia, don't you think I'm upset? I wish
  I wasn't — it doesn't give me any pleasure — but I am!
Tope (*quietly at first, his voice rising*) Miss Partington — sit down.
Miss Partington I don't want to sit down either.
Tope (*shouting*) Sit down!

The three ladies look at him in surprise: even he is surprised by his outburst

Now, I realize it's the end of term and tempers are frayed, expectations low,
but that is no reason to carry on like fishwives in the school hall. Now, Janet,
will you explain yourself, slowly and articulately, and without all these
histrionics.
Miss Partington (*quieter now*) I'm sorry, Joyce, Celia. It's just that I feel
  that if I can't do anything to help all the children, then I should concentrate
  my efforts into helping one child — Albert Nuttall.
Tope That is most praiseworthy, Janet. But how?
Miss Partington He told me just now that his mother is very ill and that she
  won't even allow a doctor into the house to see her. (*Pause*) You can't
  imagine what I've just done to that poor boy. I'd told him to pray to God
  to help him. I'd even promised that if he prayed hard enough he might even
  see God — can you believe that? But just now, when I saw the hopelessness
  in his eyes, I told him to stop praying, that it was useless, that seeing God
  was only make-believe, a tale, a fantasy to help overcome despair ...

The Lights around them fade

A pool of Light, brighter than the rest, comes up DS

Albert, breathless and excited, runs into this pool of Light

Albert (*simply, but with wonder in his voice*) I saw Him, Miss ... I saw Him
  ... I prayed hard ... ever so hard, Miss ... I screwed up my eyes like this
  and I concentrated (*he demonstrates*) just like you told me to ... and I asked
  Him to help my mum ... "Please, please," I said ... (*he opens his eyes
  again*) and just when I thought it was hopeless ... just when I thought it was
  no good ... (*a huge smile breaks out on his face*) there He was ... Miss
  Partington... you mustn't stop believing ... I saw Him, Miss ... and He was
  ... BEAUTIFULNESS!

The Light on Albert slowly fades to Black-out

ACT II

From the darkness, music

A pool of Light comes up on Albert, now in long trousers

A pool of Light comes up on Enid

A pool of Light comes up on Primrose Macaveney, now a young woman, unhappy, coarse and sad

A pool of Light comes up on Tope, Miss Hemsley, Miss Partington and Miss Mint who stand in a group together

Finally, a pool of Light, brighter than the rest, comes up DS. Miss Celia Mint walks into it

The Music fades away

Miss Mint (*cheerful as ever, speaking out front*) I lead a gay old life, children, and I'm more than content with my lot. The life of a teacher is hard: the way can be difficult, badly lit, with many knocks and bruises on the way, but, at the end of each day, in bed with a good book and my cocoa, I say to myself, "Miss Mint, Life is good" ...

Albert (*smiling*) Life is good, Miss Mint.

Miss Mint But I wasn't always a teacher, children, good heavens no — in younger days I was an actress. I appeared in plays; but it was a sorry existence and life was passing me by, until, one bleak February morning I came to Belmont Fields to work under dear Mr Tope and his troupe.

Tope (*calling across time and distance*) Children — I would like you to meet Miss Mint who will instruct you in English and the Drama ...

Everyone (*as children*) Good-morning, Miss Mint.

Miss Mint And now, children, I'm happy in life. I read, when I'm not marking your compositions, go for walks by the river, spend time in the company of my friends — you know them, children: Miss Hemsley and Miss Partington.

Miss Hemsley and Miss Partington smile at us

We visit the cinema together; the repertory theatre when the play is a nice one; trips to Hampton Court in the rain; concerts when the Hallé Orchestra is playing and, during the month of August, we travel abroad together — Venice, Rome, far-off Egypt, the outer reaches of Spain ... This year we plan to see Russia, with cardigans in case there's a chill in the air. We shall visit the Kremlin, marvel at its mystery; we have tickets booked for the opera and the ballet and the play ... Yes, children, Miss Mint has no reason to complain ... (*She stops: her dream has a bitter side: she smiles perhaps to hide her tears*) Albert Nuttall shall read you his composition. Strange but full of mystery and expectation — come, Albert, read to us.

Albert (*reading from an exercise book*) "When the sky fell down the Lord apologized. He said he was terribly sorry but that he wanted to compensate the peasants by creating a new world. He gave them towns and cities, churches for their pities, roads and streets, highways for their adventures, kindness and love for everyone to share. The peasants rejoiced and cried in this new world of the mighty one, Land of Lands, Earth of Earths. But, in a corner sat a man, all alone, with nothing to share with anyone. He looked up. Now we can jest at the disability of the many when in hindsight so few weep the song of the willow ..."

Silence. Then only Miss Mint applauds

Primrose (*across time, older now*) It made no bleedin' sense.

Miss Mint And every word correctly spelt, children ... every comma and full stop in its place, every i dotted and every t crossed. (*Proudly*) Albert Nuttall is a paragon!

Miss Mint walks away into the shadows beyond the light. Headmaster Tope moves and stands beside Albert: Miss Hemsley walks into the Light vacated by Miss Mint

Miss Hemsley (*speaking out as if in a court of law*) Enid Muriel Smallshaw, sometimes known as Enid Muriel Nuttall, of number three, Paradise Mansions, Crabtree Common, you are accused that on the thirteenth day of December you did enter the premises of Messrs Doubleday and Dawn with the intent to deprive them of one decorative brooch — value ten shillings and sixpence — fashioned in the shape of a horse's head and made from glitter and tat — and that then you did place the said brooch, unpaid for and unreceipted, into your plastic shopping bag and then did attempt to leave the shop with the stolen article, and when apprehended by store detectives (*she consults her papers*) Mr Purvis and Mr Peach, you did resist arrest and call them extremely rude names ... (*She looks out across a vast distance*) How do you plead?

Enid, tears in her eyes, confused, afraid, just stares out

Miss Hemsley (*softly, gently, kindly*) Enid? Enid? How do you plead?

Miss Hemsley walks away into the darkness. The Light on her fades

The Light on Albert and Tope grows brighter; during the following speech Albert kneels beside Tope

Tope (*harsh at first, speaking out*) The raid will take place at dawn ... When the mother leaves the house to bring the child to school several men will be there to force their way in ... It has to be done, for both their sakes; it has to be done. No-one will be harmed — I'm assured of that.

Albert reaches out and takes the Headmaster's hand

The boy trusts us, you see. He knows we intend no harm. No ordinary labels can be attached to this boy. He's no ordinary child — in fact, silly though it may sound, our Miss Partington claims him to be very spiritual, very far-seeing ...

Albert (*calling out*) I saw Him, Miss Partington. I did, Miss, I saw Him ...

Tope And I think I believe her: Miss Partington is young, yes, a little green I grant you, but she's no fool, she knows her stuff. A most gifted teacher; her faith is unshakeable, as solid as a rock ...

Miss Partington (*alone in her light, calling over to Albert*) But I don't think you could have done, Albert, it's not really possible ...

Albert (*confused*) But you said ...

Tope And Albert is no fool either: he's special ... (*there are tears in his eyes*) ... very, very special. (*He pauses. He gains control of himself*) I wish to God he'd never come to my school.

Tope exits into the darkness beyond the Light

Miss Partington comes across to join Albert in his Light; her Light fades

Enid and Primrose still remain in their own Lights

Miss Partington Forget it, Albert — please forget it.

Albert But it was like you said, Miss Partington; you said that if I prayed hard enough, He'd be there when I needed him — and He was.

Miss Partington (*sharply*) Stop it, Albert! Now, stop it at once! You saw no such thing. It was a trick of the light, an illusion — such things are not possible. (*Pause; calming herself*) You mustn't tell anyone about this,

Albert. Anyone. You understand? It could be harmful to you. They might think you're ... (*she leaves it unspoken*) It's just that here, in this world, such things never happen. I'm sorry.

She walks away slowly into the darkness

The Lights on Albert, Primrose and Enid fade to Black-out

Enid exits

Music creeps in

Lights come up to reveal the school hall. Moonlight streams in through the huge Gothic window high above

Albert and Primrose (now both 21) are embracing. Primrose's blouse is unbuttoned

Albert (*angry, confused, moving away*) No, please. NO!
Primrose (*made angry by rejection*) Oh, all right — keep your soddin' hair on. (*She starts to button up her blouse*) What are you anyway, a bleedin' puff? Albert Nuttall, you're a bloody mystery.
Albert (*quietly, distressed*) Leave me, Primrose.
Primrose We're not kids any more, Albert. I'm nearly twenty-one now. I have done it before, you know; I have got experience.
Albert I haven't — I've never done that.
Primrose I can see you haven't — but you was the first ever to look up my skirt, remember? That first day at Belmont Fields. You looked right up my skirt, you dirty little sod.

There is a pause

D'you want to know who was the first?

Albert covers his ears

(*Cruelly*) Charlie Shorrocks. Charlie Shorrocks. Behind the lockers in the changing rooms. And you know who saw us? Old Leatherbottle, Randy Dandy: he pretended he wasn't there, mind you, and we pretended he wasn't there too. We was only thirteen but we knew he was getting his kicks, the dirty sod ...
Albert (*disappointed by the passing years*) You used to be nice.
Primrose (*lighting a cigarette*) Did I?

Albert You used to be pretty, you used to wear nice frocks, you used to sing and dance, and you were on the stage — you were Jesus' mother in blue.

Primrose (*laughing at the memory*) Oh, yeah — with what's-his-name. (*Her smile fades*) He died; did you know that? We used to laugh at him — remember? — and his asthma; then, one day, he got killed on the railway near your house. (*Time has caught up — she cries softly*)

Albert (*moved, putting an arm round Primrose*) Don't cry, Primrose. Shall I kiss it better?

Primrose (*more moved by his simplicity than she dare admit*) You're a daft sod, Albert Nuttall — you are, honest.

Albert You could have been famous.

Primrose Oh, yeah?

Albert You could have been on at the theatre, singing and dancing.

Primrose A Tiller Girl? (*Again she is struck by the impact of time*) Where's Miss Mint I wonder? "You shall grow tall — like a willow — Primrose Macaveney!" (*She smiles and answers like a child*) "Yes, Miss Mint." (*Ashamed of her sentiment*) I bet she was a lesbian!

Albert You used to tap dance, with special shoes on.

Primrose (*annoyed, pushing Albert away*) Oh, leave it! All right, so I used to tap dance, but I don't friggin' tap dance any more, and I'm perfectly happy, thank you. I've got a very good job — I love it at Woolworth's. I'm in haberdashery now — I've come up in the world! (*She turns to him*) Come to bed with me, Albert Nuttall ... please! I want to be the first — you owe me that — I've been good to you and it's time for repayment ... I want your grubby body for my own before it's too late.

Albert What about Charlie?

Primrose Sod him.

Albert But you're going to marry him.

Primrose That's what I mean, Albert — it'll be too late then.

There is a long pause

Albert What do I have to do, Primrose?

Primrose (*taking his hand*) I'll make it nice — promise: I'll make it special for you.

Albert What if I don't like it?

Primrose What does that matter? Not many people do, but it's one o' them things you gotta try. You might not ever do it again, Albert, but you can always tell 'em that you did, eh? (*Pulling at his hand*) Come on, eh?

Albert Will I need to have a wash?

Primrose Oh, sod that — it's never bothered you before. Come on, before you go off the idea.

Primrose pulls him towards the exit

Albert Where?
Primrose I know just the place, come on — and when it's all over I'll do you
a tap dance … (*Giggling now, girlish again*) Eh? Eh?

  Albert and Primrose leave

*The Lights on the school hall fade. Music fills the air. The Lights come up on
the Headmaster's study. We are back in the past*

Tope is seated at his desk. Miss Hemsley is standing, full of excitement

*Eric Smallshaw is sitting on a chair somewhat distant from the desk. He is
very dirty, shabby and simple; now, and at all times, he carries a grubby
brown paper parcel done up with string*

The music fades

Miss Hemsley (*excited*) It's a breakthrough, Headmaster.
Tope (*staring at Eric Smallshaw*) Who is it … he?
Miss Hemsley (*to Eric*) Tell the Headmaster your name. Your name, man.
Eric Smallshaw, Eric Leslie Smallshaw, at your service, Sir.
Tope (*bewildered*) Well?
Miss Hemsley Do you not see the resemblance? The family likeness?
Tope To whom?
Miss Hemsley To Albert and Enid Nuttall.
Eric She ain't called Nuttall. Not ever in this world, Missis.
Miss Hemsley Miss. Miss Hemsley. Health and Social Welfare, Division
Three!
Tope You mean … this is … ?
Miss Hemsley The mother's brother, Mr Tope. I've searched everywhere,
high and low, and he just turns up out of the blue.
Eric (*clutching his parcel*) From the Bush.
Tope Australia?
Eric No. Shepherd's Bush. I've been doing a little job there, see? In the toilets
an' that, see? But they laid me off, the council, 'cos o' my back, see? I'm
Eric Smallshaw, see?
Tope I'm sorry, Miss Hemsley, but I fail to see ——
Miss Hemsley But, Headmaster, all is now well, no need to break down
doors, no need for unsightly violence now — Mr Smallshaw here can do
it all for us.
Tope But how?

Miss Hemsley Mr Smallshaw, tell him.

Eric (*confused*) Wot?

Miss Hemsley You want to come back, don't you? To the family home —
number three, Paradise Mansions?

Eric Yeah, well, it's my home, see.

Tope But he's been away nearly fifteen years.

Miss Hemsley What does that matter?

Tope (*trying not to be overheard by Eric*) But — he seems no better, no
cleaner.

Eric Pardon, Mister?

Tope Why have you suddenly decided to come back, Mr Smallshaw?

Eric I've lost my job, see, I've been redundified: the bleeders sacked me.
"Piss off," they said, "Get lost!". And I had my little room, didn't I? Like
a palace it was: clean sheets once a fortnight, no smoking in bed! I tell you
it was like a palace, not like how that dirty cow lived — my sister, dirty cow
she is, talk about pong! — never took a bar of soap to herself. I used to say,
"It's no way to live, girl," I used to say.

Tope (*unhappy*) Miss Hemsley, I'm sure my study is no place for all this ...
I'm a headmaster, all this is no concern of mine; I have a school to run here.

Miss Hemsley But Albert, Mr Tope — what about Albert?

Tope (*rising, trying to reason*) But lines have to be drawn somewhere, Joyce.
This man may confuse the issue, just when we had everything sorted. The
men from the corporation will be there tomorrow morning; I've given my
permission.

Miss Hemsley But you yourself said you hated doing that.

Tope Well, I do, Joyce, believe me I do. But it will be over, done with; Albert
will be safe and able to lead a normal life. And now — this!

Eric Wot's he mean, Missis?

Tope (*to Hemsley*) You see my dilemma, surely?

Miss Hemsley (*tetchy now*) I'm sorry, I seem to have done the wrong thing
again. I'm very sorry.

Tope Now, please don't take offence, Joyce, I don't think I can cope with
that. (*To Eric*) Look, Mr Smallshaw — Eric — I wonder if you'd mind
waiting elsewhere for a moment ... ?

Eric Perhaps I could see little Albert.

Tope Well, yes, yes, of course. You'll find him out in our little farmyard with
our Miss Partington; they feed the beasts. (*He shows Eric to the door*)
Perhaps you could ... (*He covers his mouth with a handkerchief to avoid
the smell*)

Eric (*meaning Miss Hemsley*) I hope I haven't ...

Tope No, no, I'm quite sure you haven't ... goodbye, Mr Smallshaw ...

Eric (*leaving*) Eric Leslie ...

Eric exits muttering

Tope Now, Joyce — do pull yourself together. I wish to God I'd never met Albert Nuttall or his wretched family.

Miss Hemsley You know who that man is, don't you?

Tope You've just told me — her brother.

Miss Hemsley (*with much deeper meaning*) Yes.

Tope Joyce, you are talking in double meanings; how am I expected to know anything if I'm never sure what you're talking about? Now, please!

Miss Hemsley (*quieter now*) That man is also Albert's father.

Silence

Tope (*unable to let it sink in*) His ... (*He sits, ashen*) Oh, no ... (*He leaves a long pause*) How long have you known?

Miss Hemsley I've suspected it for some time. She once said something that made me think she used to sleep in the same bed as him.

Tope (*obviously putting two and two together*) Just as now she sleeps with her son: my God — you don't think ... ?

Miss Hemsley It seems strange to me who has never known love, that that poor, simple woman should have known so much.

Tope Good God, what are you saying, Joyce?

Miss Hemsley Whatever you say, it is love. Do you realize that from the day she was born that woman has never gone to bed without someone to hold her tight: her parents, her brother, and now her son. How do we make her see that all that is wrong?

Tope But it is wrong, and you know it. It's hideous.

Miss Hemsley Yes. I suppose it is. But I've never been to bed with anyone, Headmaster. Not ever. Not in the whole of my life.

There is a pause

Tope (*knowing he has not either*) Yes, well — we were born on another side of the park, Miss Hemsley.

The Lights slowly fade to Black-out

Music and the sound of birds and farmyard noise

The Lights come up on a small farmyard

Miss Partington is quietly marking books. Albert, now in long trousers, is feeding the pigs. They are both at their happiest

Miss Partington Careful, Albert — he'll bite you. Pigs do bite when they get cross.

Albert (*holding his nose*) Oh, Miss — he's just made a fart, Miss. Stinky-stinky-poos. (*Amazed by the sight*) Look, Miss, look at him now — he's shitted!

Miss Partington (*laughing but trying not to*) Albert! You'll get us into trouble. He's defecated, Albert.

Albert (*still looking, excited*) Look, he's defecated again, Miss. Does defecated mean he's shitted, Miss?

Miss Partington Something like that. (*She looks at her watch*) It'll soon be break time.

Albert Does that mean we've got to go, Miss?

Miss Partington I'm afraid so.

Albert Can we come back after playtime?

Miss Partington No. I've got to teach the first years. This is my free lesson; I'm not free all the time.

Albert Do the first years behave good, Miss?

Miss Partington Yes. But not for long. They soon realize that in my lesson they can scream and shout and draw rude things in my books.

Albert Is that because you're not a very good teacher, Miss? (*He throws food to the pig*)

Miss Partington I suppose it must be, Albert. (*She watches him*)

Albert You can't make a noise in Mr Ram's class, Miss. Or Miss Mint's. They don't like it. Miss Mint rolls down your socks and slaps your legs and goes "Naughty, naughty, naughty!" — like that.

Miss Partington And do they hate Miss Mint for doing that?

Albert Oh, no. Nobody hates Miss Mint. She's funny. She makes you laugh with her silly stories. Like me.

Miss Partington What do you mean? Like you?

Albert I make people laugh.

Miss Partington How do you know?

Albert Because Primrose Macaveney told me, Miss. And my mum. Sometimes when my mum is very sad she calls me, "Albert Make Us Laugh"; she does, Miss.

Miss Partington And do you? Make her laugh?

Albert Yes.

Miss Partington How?

Albert I just tell her about things, everyday things, what happens at school — she's never been to school, you see — so she doesn't know how funny it can be.

Miss Partington But everyone has to go to school, Albert. It's the law.

Albert Well, my Mummy Enid didn't — and she didn't go to prison, Miss. (*He pauses*) Is it the law that makes you come to school, Miss?

Miss Partington (*laughing*) No. I don't have to come if I don't want to.

Albert Then why do you, Miss? 'Cos you don't like it, do you?

Miss Partington (*looking at him*) How do you know?
Albert I can tell.
Miss Partington (*changing the subject*) The sun's hot today.
Albert Are you happy like me, Miss?
Miss Partington (*smiling at him*) I'm happy. Just like you, Albert.

An awkward pause: Miss Partington looks away

Albert Could I come to your house?
Miss Partington (*feeling awkward*) Well ... I suppose you could — if you really wanted to.
Albert I'd like that. (*He stares at her*) I would like that, Miss Partington.

Any other fourteen-year-old boy would cause her embarrassment but somehow she feels that Albert shouldn't; however, she is fully aware of the way he is looking at her

During the following, almost ominously, Eric Smallshaw appears in the distance behind Albert and Miss Partington, and stands watching them, his brown paper parcel in his hand

Miss Partington (*after a moment's thought*) Well, I'm sure we could arrange it.
Albert Do you live with your mummy and daddy or with a husband like Mrs Tucker and Mrs Schofield?
Miss Partington No. No, Albert: I live alone.
Eric (*calling over, shading his eyes from the sun*) Hi, there.

Albert and Miss Partington turn to see Eric

Miss Partington I'm sorry. This is private property. Can I help?
Eric (*calling*) Sorry?
Miss Partington (*seeing only an old tramp*) You're on school property — you can't come in.
Eric Miss Partington?
Miss Partington (*puzzled*) Yes.
Eric They said I'd find you here. The Head. Mr Tope.
Miss Partington What do you want?
Eric I'd like to see *him*.
Miss Partington Who? Albert?
Eric Yes. The boy. Albert. I'd like to see him.
Miss Partington Albert — do you know this man?
Albert No, Miss. (*He turns away to feed the pig*)

Eric (*persisting*) We's related, see, Miss. Him and me — we's related.
Miss Partington (*unsure*) Well, I suppose you could see him — but only for
    a moment.
Eric (*coming towards them*) Gawd bless you, Miss.
Miss Partington (*gathering her books together and rising*) Albert, I shall
    be just over there if you need me.

Still unsure about Eric, Miss Partington exits

*Silence. Eric watches Albert feed the animals. Albert doesn't look at Eric at
all*

Eric Coo — wot a pong!
Albert Defecated.
Eric Oh, yeah. (*After a long pause*) Nice out here. Nice.
Albert Are you a teacher? You don't look like a teacher.
Eric No. I ain't a teacher. You're a big lad, Albert. You must be ... how old?
Albert I'm nearly — fifteen, I think.
Eric (*with a toothless laugh*) You think! You mean you're not sure? (*To
    himself*) Bleedin' silly like his mum. (*He pauses, watching Albert*) Know
    who I am, do you?
Albert No.
Eric How's your silly mother? How's Enid?

Albert turns to Eric for the first time and looks at him long and hard

Albert My mum's OK. Who are you?

*The Lights fade and come up on Albert's home. Enid, in her new nightie, is
playing with her dolls on the bed*

A train thunders past

Albert and Eric, who still clutches his parcel, become part of the scene

Albert (*moving to Enid*) Mummy, look, he came to school ...

*Enid sees Eric. She is terrified. She quickly hides her dolls away; her world
is shattered*

Enid What's he want?
Albert (*innocently*) He's Uncle Eric.
Enid I don't want him here. What's he want?

Eric (*smiling unpleasantly*) Hallo, Enid, girl.

Enid I don't want you here; he'd no right to bring you.

Eric Aw, shut it! Whingeing. This is my home, in't it?

Albert He came to my school, Mummy — he saw Miss Partington. He said
he was Uncle Eric. (*Seeing Enid's fear*) Mummy?

Enid Play with your jigsaw, Albert.

Albert I've finished it. It had three pieces missing.

Enid (*sharply*) Do it again.

Albert, puzzled by Enid's anger, moves into the shadows of the room

Eric He's grown up nice. Pity he's daft; runs in the family it seems.

Enid Please go away, we don't want you here. We don't want anybody here.

Eric Oh, but they're relying on me. Mr Tope and his mates had a few serious
words with me, Enid — they're depending on me to help 'em out. I've got
back in the nick of time by the looks of things.

Enid (*loudly*) Get away from us.

Eric They look on you as a bit of a headache, an eyesore, Enid, a blot on the
bleedin' landscape. No, they're relieved I'm back I can assure you. "Mr
Smallshaw", they said, "we're relying on you," they said.

Enid Frig off! Go! Leave us alone!

Eric (*calling over to Albert*) Here — you hear this, Albert? Can you hear this
mouthful she's coming out with? You enjoy your jigsaw, son ... ignore this
foul-mouthed cow here. (*To Enid*) You wanna watch your bleedin'
language in front of the boy.

Enid is helpless. She kneels on the bed, twisting and untwisting a blanket

Enid (*a cry deep from within*) Please, please, somebody help me.

Eric You're beyond help, girl, you're way beyond help; they're coming to
put you away, Enid. You're straight off your bleedin' trolley you are, girl.

Enid You left me — you went away — you left me.

Eric Well, of course I left; what else could I do? You was a very naughty girl,
Enid. I loved you, I took care of you — didn't I?

Enid You — you — touched me; you swore you'd never do that but you
touched me — here. You gave me Albert — and then you left me.

Eric Leave off whingeing: leave it out.

Enid I had nobody here to help me. I was big with him. Things started
happening to my body — pains. I lay on this bed for days. Nobody came.
I didn't know about babies. I didn't eat — days I didn't eat.

Albert (*distressed*) Mummy ... ? (*He crawls along the floor and holds his
mother around her legs*)

Enid One day the pain got bad again, very bad. I called and called but you never came. I sweated, I cooled myself with water. A lady came — from over the way — she heard me crying; she helped me and he came ... (*she holds on to Albert*) from my stomach — and he loved me.

Silence. In her simple distress Enid clings to her son

Eric (*moved for the first time*) I can help you, Enid, I can help, see. They wanna take him from you — but old Eric won't let 'em, see?

Enid, hopeful now, looks at her brother for help

I can help you ... I don't see why I should, mind ... but I can ... get it?
Enid Please. Oh, please, Eric.
Eric If I come back and live with you, they'll find us a nice house — the corporation, see? A nice house, with grass and a garden. And a bathroom, Enid. You see, I've grown accustomed to such things in my new life in Shepherd's Bush, see. I led the life of a friggin' lord in Shepherd's Bush. You know pig all, Enid, you've been left out, but I can put you on the stairway to heaven, girl — BUT!
Enid (*eager, childlike*) But what? Tell me.
Eric (*grabbing Enid's arm, twisting it up her back*) You gotta stop arseholing about, girl. And you can't go telling them nosey sods that I put you up the spout — see?
Enid But I never have, Eric, I never told nobody, not a soul.
Eric Sure? I can always find out. I have my methods, girl.
Enid Never, I swear to it, Eric. That's why I called us Nuttall, see? So as they'd think I was a married widow — see? (*She smiles*) I'm not daft.
Eric No? Bleedin' scotch mist, is it?

Enid starts to laugh; so does Eric. Albert, unsure why, starts to laugh as well

And, Enid, do have a wash; we can't turn up at Orchard View Estate looking like piggin' gypsies ...

A train whistle blows outside. The Lights fade to Black-out

The stage is cleared completely

Music fills the theatre. A pool of very bright white Light comes up c of the bare stage

Albert and Janet Partington walk into the light from opposite sides of the stage. Without words, as simply and as beautifully as possible, Albert starts to unbutton her blouse. They embrace

The Light and the music slowly fade

Another pool of light comes up DL *and Eric Smallshaw and Tope walk into it*

Eric (*oily, into Tope's ear*) It's a hopeless case, Mr Tope. I've pleaded with my sister — on my bended knees I was — "Enid," I said, "That dear Mr Tope wants to help you," I said — but it's useless. Too far gone, see, Sir, lives entirely in a world of her own. She nicks stuff from the Self-Service; granted it's only food for her and that boy, but I'm embarrassed, Mr Tope, embarrassed out of my wits. You see I led a normal sort of life in the Bush; I've learned the rules of the game, see, and I adhere to them very, very strictly — but Enid —— (*A sharp intake of breath*)
Tope (*distressed*) Oh dear, oh dear ...
Eric St Botolph's? The East Wing? I know what you're thinking, Sir ... and you mustn't blame yourself.

Tope moves to go but Eric stops him

(*More poison*) And the boy, Sir — I hope I'm not speaking out of turn — but that young bit of stuff on your staff — Miss Partington, is it? — I think she's in the habit of getting Albert round her house, know what I mean ...?

Tope's face is a study in horror

Black-out

Lights come up on Miss Mint's classroom: she is putting things away

Miss Hemsley enters

Both teachers are a little downcast but try not to show it

Miss Hemsley Coast clear, dear?
Miss Mint Ahh, Joyce — come in. Thank God it's Friday.

They sit

Miss Hemsley (*with a sigh*) Yes. The river? The library? Church?
Miss Mint Suddenly it all sounds very dull. You?
Miss Hemsley The vet.
Miss Mint Not the dogs.

Miss Hemsley I was prepared. Don't comfort me, Celia, please. I shall only burst into tears. They're only bloody dogs and they'll have to be put down sooner or later. They're older than I am for God's sake!

Miss Mint Well, I'm sorry, dear.

Silence. The two women just stare into space

Miss Mint (*hardly daring to ask*) Any news?

Miss Hemsley No. She was still in there when I asked. (*She offers Miss Mint a mint*) Polo?

Miss Mint (*taking one*) Thanks. (*She holds the mint up*) You know, I'm sure the hole gets bigger, Joyce.

Silence. They suck their mints

I thought we'd go to Mozambique next year.

Miss Hemsley (*not really interested*) Mozambique. (*She pauses*) Where is it?

Miss Mint I've no idea. Ask Mr Ram. He'll know. But it sounds rather exotic — don't you think? (*Savouring the sound of it*) Mozambique!

Miss Hemsley I'm sure it's Africa — that way on. (*After a long pause*) Do you often wonder if life has passed us by, Celia?

Miss Mint I wouldn't know, Joyce. I've seen more of it than you, I dare say. (*She pauses*) I was married once, you know.

Miss Hemsley (*dumbfounded*) Celia! You never were. I've known you all these years and you've never said.

Miss Mint Oh the rare occasions that I remembered it didn't seem worth mentioning somehow.

Miss Hemsley You're a dark horse, Celia, and I may never speak to you again. We have travelled the globe together in search of experience and you never ever told me you'd been married.

Miss Mint Forget I ever did, dear. (*Pause*) His name was Vivian and he was a pale shade of puce.

Miss Hemsley Good God! Heart?

Miss Mint No, dear. Drink. Gallons of it.

Miss Hemsley Did he die?

Miss Mint Not while I was with him — thankfully.

Miss Hemsley And did he ... ?

Miss Mint I'm not going to tell you any more, Joyce, so you needn't ask.

Janet Partington appears. She is packed and ready to leave

Janet, dear — how are you?

Miss Partington I've come to say goodbye.

Miss Mint Good God in heaven — they haven't!

Miss Partington I'm afraid they have. But I'm fine. Really. The school board were far more embarrassed than me. The vicar's wife nearly passed out — they had to give her water. (*She sits, tired, worn*) May I? Just for a moment.

Miss Mint (*concerned*) Oh, my dear. (*She puts her arm around Janet*)

Joyce Hemsley stands at a distance, her head bent

Well, at least it's all over — you can say good riddance to this place for ever.

Miss Partington And to teaching. I'm afraid they made it clear that I shall never work in this profession again.

Miss Hemsley (*uneasy*) Excuse me, I really must go.

Miss Partington Joyce — please don't go like that.

Miss Hemsley I'm sorry, Janet, but I can't say I'm surprised you've been given the sack — and I really can't stand here and be two-faced about it.

Miss Partington No-one wants you to be two-faced, Joyce. I'd simply like you to say goodbye.

Miss Hemsley (*filing up with tears*) Goodbye — and good luck. (*She tries to hurry away*)

Miss Mint (*firmly*) Joyce Hemsley — come back here at once! Or are you a bigger bloody coward than I took you for?

Miss Partington Leave her, Celia.

Miss Mint I will not leave her. Do you think I could ever go on holiday again with a — a turncoat!

Miss Hemsley That woman is a molester of children, Celia. I cannot be in the same room with her.

Miss Mint Oh, sit down, you silly woman. What harm has she done? She probably did the poor boy more good than a thousand of my boring old English lessons.

Miss Hemsley Celia! How can you stand there and talk like that?

Miss Mint I'll shout it from the roof if you like. Now, if you or I had been to bed with Albert Nuttall ——

Miss Hemsley (*whispering*) Keep your voice down ...

Miss Partington I did *not* go to bed with him. There was nothing sordid or dirty: we simply held each other close, nothing more than that. That's what I told them in there, but of course they wouldn't begin to understand. It wasn't sex, or lust, it was pure joy; the kind I never knew existed.

Miss Hemsley (*such words only embarrass her*) I'm sorry, but I can't stand here and listen to this. Perhaps in time, when things have blown over ... (*She weeps*) ... I'm sorry, Janet, you'll just have to accept my good wishes — and I shall miss you very much.

She rushes from the room in tears, handkerchief to mouth

Headmaster Tope enters

Tope Ah, Miss Mint, if I might have just a word ... ? Is Joyce Hemsley upset?
Miss Mint I'm afraid saying goodbye to Miss Partington was more than she
could bear.
Tope (*uncomfortable*) Ah, well, yes. Unpleasant business. I do hope you're
not too downhearted, Janet?
Miss Partington I'm fine, thank you, Headmaster.
Tope (*kindly*) I would like you to know I did my best for you in there.
Miss Partington (*sincerely*) I know you did — and I'm very grateful.
Tope Perhaps if it had been anyone other than — that boy.
Miss Partington Oh, you mean they'd have forgiven me seducing any other
boy?
Tope (*wounded*) That is not what I meant.

Janet doesn't reply

Miss Mint, if you could — in my study, perhaps.
Miss Mint Of course. I'm not going to say goodbye, Janet. I realize you need
time to think, dear. But if you should need me — you know the number.

Celia Mint exits quietly

Tope I'm afraid I'm not awfully good at this kind of thing, but I would like
to thank you for all you've done at Belmont Fields. I wish you well and
hope, very sincerely, that you will, in time, find your heart's desire.

There is a silence

Tope knows there is nothing more to say; he exits

*Left alone, Janet Partington sits for a moment then starts to gather her things
together*

Albert enters

Ready to leave, Janet turns to take one last look about her and notices Albert

Miss Partington (*after a long silence*) Hallo, Albert. I'm sorry, but I don't
know what to say.

Albert is silent

All I know, Albert, is that whatever I do, wherever I go, I shall never forget you.

She looks at him for a while, then, simply, turns and walks off

There is silence; then music creeps in. The Lights fade, then come up dimly on Albert's home. Enid is (or appears to be) asleep in bed. Eric Smallshaw is asleep on the floor, using his brown paper parcel as a pillow

The music fades and a train whistle blows at a distance

Albert goes and lies on the bed beside his mother

We hear the sound of glass breaking

Headmaster Tope, dressed now in overcoat, hat and scarf, enters with Miss Hemsley, who is also dressed for the street. They have obviously smashed a window to get into the house

Tope (*seeing the appalling squalor*) Good God … !
Miss Hemsley I told you what to expect …
Tope Open a window, Joyce, for heaven's sake.
Miss Hemsley Have you cut yourself?
Tope It's nothing much.
Miss Hemsley Iodine and a bandage when we get back; there won't be any here.
Tope I feel like a criminal, Joyce. I've never broken into anything before, not anything.
Miss Hemsley (*seeing Smallshaw*) Well, at least he's not in the bed as well. (*Kicking Eric*) Mr Smallshaw, Mr Smallshaw, come along, day has dawned — the time has come for flitting.
Eric (*waking with a start; half asleep*) I didn't do it; the bleeders pinned it on me … (*He realizes where he is*) Jesus Christ — it's a woman!
Miss Hemsley Not a woman, Mr Smallshaw: Miss Hemsley, Health and Social Welfare. Fear not, Mr Tope and I have come to see you get moved quite safely to Orchard View.
Tope (*raising his hat*) Good-morning, Smallshaw.
Eric Why you two? Not a Headmaster's job is this.
Miss Hemsley Either us or twelve burly brutes from the corporation — and we didn't wish to put Albert through all that! How is he?
Eric Not bad; poor fucker gets confused with it all — sorry, missis, no offence. She's been bad, though, in the night, coughing, catching her breath like.

Miss Hemsley There are such things as doctors, you know. (*She moves to the bed*). Albert, come along, dear: today is the start of your new adventure. Enid?

We see that Albert is awake with his arms around his dead mother

Tope What is it?

Joyce turns Enid over and sees her dead staring eyes

Oh, my God! Is she … ?
Miss Hemsley Shhh! Let's get Albert out of here …

During Eric's following speech, Tope helps Albert out of bed, puts his arms around him and leads him out

Miss Hemsley tidies the bed, covers Enid with a sheet etc. then leaves

Eric (*seemingly unaware of anything*) I won't have a wash straight away, I'll wait till we get to Orchard View. Course, in the Bush I had hot running water an' everything: shoes polished, waitin' on the mat when you opened the door; breakfast on the table, toast — brown or white, whatever took your fancy — Kellogg's with cold milk, fresh from the cow, two colours of jam. You see, I'm used to the finer things in life. I mean, living in shit like this — well, I ask you — but don't worry about the new place, I'll keep it spick an' span. Proper little palace it'll be: we'll get a Hoover, a little second-hand job, and a plug for the wall; clean nets at the windows … (*He begins to cry; he is lost, lonely*) … house proud I'll be; the smell of Ibcol of a Saturday morning, like when me an' her was kids. Spotless it'll be, not like that dirty cow, not like our Enid … (*He sits, clutching his parcel, tears running down his face*)

The room is silent; just Eric and his dead sister

The Lights slowly fade on Albert's home

In the darkness the voice of Primrose Macaveney echoes through the theatre

Primrose's Voice Albert? … Albert? … Albert Nuttall … ?

Moonlight floods the stage through a Gothic window with the brightest part c. We are back in the school hall

Primrose comes running on, her clothes in disarray

Primrose (*breathless, scared, half laughing, half afraid of the dark*) Albert?
Albert, don't mess about — Albert, please!

Albert makes a spooky noise, off

(*Scared*) Albert — now stop it! Is that you? It's not funny any more.

*Albert enters, his braces down and fly buttons undone; he creeps up behind
Primrose and jumps at her*

Albert BOO!!!
Primrose (*terrified*) Jesus — you silly sod, Albert. You nearly frit the shit
out of me there.

*Albert, a virgin no longer, is on top of the world. He starts to tickle
Primrose. They laugh and fall on the floor*

(*Helpless with laughter*) Gerroff! Albert, I'm going to smash you if you
don't ...

They calm down and sit together c where the Light is brightest

Primrose You haven't got a Woodbine have you?
Albert No. Why?
Primrose You don't know nothing, do you? You're supposed to have a
Woodbine after sex — like Googie Withers.
Albert Who's Googie Withers?
Primrose She's on the pictures: she's a very famous film star. She always
has a smoke after she's been at it. Charlie Shorrocks always gives me a
Woodbine after we've done it. You're bleedin' useless, Albert Nuttall.
Albert Was I better than Charlie, Primrose?
Primrose Well, I don't know about that. You made less noise than he does,
I must say — he goes at it like the trains past your old house ...

Albert looks downcast

(*Taking Albert's hand; sincerely*) You were smashin', Albert, honest. Just
look at the state of you. Do your fly up ... you'll have it all poppin' out.
Albert (*with a cheeky grin*) Would you like that?
Primrose Here, you better watch it: just because you've had one go doesn't
mean you've got to go raving mad.
Albert Can we do it again?
Primrose What — now?

Albert Oh no, I couldn't do it now. (*He does up his fly buttons*) It's gone to sleep for the night. But soon, eh?

Primrose (*a bit depressed*) How can we? I'm getting married to Charlie aren't I? Don't you know anything?

Albert No.

Primrose You gotta stay faithful for ever and ever when you get married, you gotta promise on the Bible an' that. I gotta stand in that registry office next week and I gotta say, "I love you Charlie Shorrocks, for ever and ever, in sickness, in health, for richer for poorer, till death us do part", an' all that, see?

Albert Cor, that's a lot. Is it serious?

Primrose Course it's serious, it's marriage, in't it?

Albert And do you? Love him, Primrose. Do you love Charlie?

Primrose (*looking away, unsure*) Yeah, 'course I do.

There is silence: she is looking away, he at her

But I love you best. (*She turns to him*)

Albert is lost, not sure what it all means

Albert Is that love? What we just done behind the lockers?

Primrose No, you daft thing. Anybody can do that. Animals do that, that's nothing special; it doesn't mean you love each other, see. Love is like when you're very, very hungry, or when you want a drink of water; it's a feeling you get in the pit of your stomach. (*She pauses, then looks at him*) Have you never had it?

Albert I'm not sure ... I don't think so.

Primrose (*with a touch of jealousy perhaps*) Do you remember Miss Partington?

Albert Who?

Primrose Oh, come off it — Miss Partington, at school. You liked her — remember?

Albert looks out into space for a long time. He looks distant: does he remember or not?

Albert No. I don't remember.

Primrose (*quietly*) Oh. I see.

Albert I don't like to remember things, Primrose, and I don't like to look forward either; things never happen the way you want them to. I like today best. I feel very safe when it's today; then it's always nice. You always know where you are when it's today; today's very special — like just now.

There is a long pause

I always thought you might get married to me.

Primrose (*moved*) I can't do that, Albert. But I love you very much, Albert Nuttall.

Albert So I won't see you again.

Primrose (*quietly*) No.

There is a silence. Neither looks at the other. After a while a smile starts to play around Primrose's mouth: that old twinkle comes back into her eyes

Here ... what do you do on Thursdays?

Albert Thursdays? I go to work, Primrose.

Primrose No, Albert, during the evening — Thursday nights?

Albert (*thinking about it for a while then cottoning on; cheekily*) Nuffink ... why?

Primrose Well, I'm not saying anything but he has his darts on a Thursday, and Charlie would never miss his darts.

Albert What about it?

Primrose Oh, Jesus, Albert: you know, sometimes I think you put it on — nobody's that bleedin' slow.

Albert (*his face aglow*) You mean ... we could ... ?

Primrose (*pretending to be coy now*) Here — don't you go getting any ideas.

They both start to laugh

Albert (*a sudden thought*) Here — you forgot.

Primrose What?

Albert You promised something — remember?

Primrose (*rising to leave*) I promised nothing. Come on, before we get caught in here.

Albert (*grabbing her arm*) Oh, no, you said that when we'd — you know — when we'd ——

Primrose Oh, do get on with it — what?

Albert You said you'd do a tap dance for me.

Primrose Oh, do leave it out. You wore me out. A girl can't do what I've just done then get up and friggin' tap dance, honest, you know nothing, Albert Nuttall ...

He only has to smile that smile of his

Oh, all right, but if you think I'm going to do this every Thursday night — you've got another think coming ... .

In her pool of Light, Primrose Macaveney starts to dance

Offstage we hear the children singing "Vote, vote, vote for Albert Nuttall ... "

   As at the beginning of the play the cast enter dressed as children

Primrose dances

Children   Vote, vote, vote for Albert Nuttall,
                    Vote for him because he's daft,
                    Albert is the one — if you need a bit of fun,
                    And you'll all feel better 'cos you laughed!

The song builds and is repeated. Albert laughs. The Lights get brighter and brighter. Suddenly everybody freezes

   Headmaster Tope enters

Tope Here at Belmont Fields we all start on the floor. In our second year we sit on the PT benches, in our third on the grown-up chairs, and in our fourth and final year we stand at the back of the hall with our legs one foot apart and our hands clasped modestly in front. Good-morning, boys and girls of Belmont Fields.
Everyone Good-morning, Headmaster!

Black-out

FURNITURE AND PROPERTY LIST

ACT I

On stage: Nil

Off stage: Push-chair for **Albert** (**Enid**)
Chairs and desks, paper, rubbers, books, etc. (**Children**)
School report (**Tope**)
Flask, box of sandwiches, napkin (**Shane**)
Woodbine (**Charlie**)
Bar of chocolate (**Enid**)
Lunch on tray (**Tope**)

Personal: **Tope**: whistle
Miss Mint: apple
Miss Hemsley: handkerchief

During black-out p. 23-24

Set: ALBERT'S HOME SETTING
Double bed
Chest of drawers. *In a drawer*: brown paper parcel containing bar of
    soap, bottle of shampoo, nightie
Rag dolls
Bowl of water
Pyjamas

During black-out p. 26

Strike: All the above

During black-out p. 28-29

Set: Large wicker property basket
Assortment of properties

ACT II

On stage: Exercise book for **Albert**

Off stage: Exercise books, pen (**Miss Partington**)
                  Luggage (**Miss Partington**)

Personal: **Eric**: brown paper parcel
                  Miss Hemsley: tube of Polos, handkerchief

During black-out p. 38

Set: Desk for **Tope**
                  Chair for **Eric**

During black-out p. 40

Strike: Desk and chair

During black-out p. 43

Set: ALBERT'S HOME SETTING
                  Double bed
                  Chest of drawers
                  Rag dolls

During black-out p. 45

Strike: All the above

During black-out p. 46

Set: Items for **Miss Mint** to put away

During black-out p.50

Strike: **Miss Mint**'s items

Set: ALBERT'S HOME SETTING
                  Double bed
                  Chest of drawers

LIGHTING PLOT

Property fittings required: nil. Various simple interior and exterior settings

To open: Darkness

ACT I

Cue 1	Music *Bring up lights on school hall; sunny morning effect*	(Page 1)
Cue 2	The cast freeze *Fade lights on school hall slightly; bring up pool of light* DR	(Page 6)
Cue 3	**Hemsley**: "The mother's called ... " *Bring up light on* **Enid**	(Page 6)
Cue 4	**Hemsley**: "The woman is also a thief!" *Fade lights on* **Enid** *and* DR; *brighten lights on school hall*	(Page 7)
Cue 5	**Children** (*singing*) "Vote ... for Albert Nuttall." *Fade all lights except pool on* **Albert**	(Page 8)
Cue 6	**Albert** runs off *Bring up lights on classroom; establish children* *impersonating helicopters, then fade* **Albert**'*s light*	(Page 9)
Cue 7	The cast freeze *Cross-fade lights to pool* DL	(Page 11)
Cue 8	**Enid** and **Tope** walk away *Cross-fade lights to classroom*	(Page 11)
Cue 9	**Albert**'s voice begins to echo *Bring up spot on* **Albert** *and dim classroom*	(Page 14)
Cue 10	**Miss Mint**: " ... something must be done." *Black-out*	(Page 15)
Cue 11	Playground sounds *Bring up lights on playground*	(Page 15)
Cue 12	Music *Fade background lights except warm pool on* **Albert**	(Page 19)

Cue 13   **Albert** and **Enid** hold each other with great affection   (Page 19)
             Bring up lights on Headmaster's study

Cue 14   **Miss Hemsley** takes **Enid** in her arms   (Page 22)
             Fade lights to black-out

Cue 15   Whistle blows   (Page 22)
             Bring up lights on sports hall

Cue 16   **Charlie** shows his bum   (Page 23)
             Black-out

Cue 17   Sound of train rushing past   (Page 24)
             Bring up lights on **Albert***'s Home setting*

Cue 18   **Enid**: "Nothing at all." *Silence*   (Page 25)
             Dim lights on **Albert***'s Home setting*

Cue 19   **Enid** holds the nightdress against herself   (Page 26)
             Fade lights to black-out

Cue 20   Music: "Silent Night"   (Page 26)
             Bring up bright ring of light DR

Cue 21   **Miss Partington** looks up   (Page 26)
             Cross-fade to **Miss Partington***'s classroom*

Cue 22   **Miss Partington**: " ... it's a waste of time."   (Page 28)
             The lights fade

Cue 23   Music: Christmas Carol   (Page 28)
             Bring up bright "stage" lights on school hall setting

Cue 24   **Miss Partington**: " ... a fantasy to help overcome despair ... "(Page 32)
             Cross-fade to pool of light DS

Cue 25   **Albert**: " ... BEAUTIFULNESS!"   (Page 32)
             Slowly fade light on **Albert** *to black-out*

ACT II

To open: Darkness

Cue 26   Music: when ready   (Page 33)
             Bring up lights one by one, on **Albert***;* **Enid***;*
             Primrose, Tope, Miss Hemsley, Miss Partington
             and **Miss Mint***: then a brighter pool* DS

Cue 27	**Miss Hemsley** walks into the darkness *Fade light on* **Miss Hemsley***; bring up light on* **Albert** *and* **Tope**	(Page 35)
Cue 28	**Miss Partington** joins **Albert** in his light *Fade lights on* **Miss Partington***'s area as she leaves it*	(Page 35)
Cue 29	**Miss Partington** walks away into the darkness *Fade lights on* **Albert***,* **Primrose** *and* **Enid**	(Page 36)
Cue 30	Music *Bring up lights on school hall setting with moonlight effect*	(Page 36)
Cue 31	**Albert** and **Primrose** leave *Fade lights to black-out*	(Page 38)
Cue 32	Music *Bring up lights on headmaster's study*	(Page 38)
Cue 33	**Tope**: " ... another side of the park, Miss Hemsley." *Slowly fade lights to black-out*	(Page 40)
Cue 34	Music; birds; farmyard noises *Bring up lights on farmyard setting*	(Page 40)
Cue 35	**Albert**: "Who are you?" *Cross-fade to* **Albert***'s Home setting*	(Page 43)
Cue 36	Train whistle blows *Fade lights to black-out*	(Page 45)
Cue 37	Music *Bring up pool of very bright light* c	(Page 45)
Cue 38	**Albert** and **Miss Partington** embrace *Cross-fade pool of light* c *to pool of light* DL	(Page 46)
Cue 39	**Tope**'s face is a study in horror *Black-out; bring up light on* **Miss Mint***'s classroom*	(Page 46)
Cue 40	Music *Cross-fade to dim lighting on* **Albert***'s Home setting*	(Page 50)
Cue 41	After a silence *Slowly fade lights on* **Albert***'s Home setting*	(Page 50)
Cue 42	**Primrose's Voice**: " ... Albert Nuttall ...?" *Bring up moonlight effect; brightest part* c	(Page 51)

| *Cue* 43 | The song is repeated; **Albert** laughs
Increase brightness of lights | (Page 55) |
| *Cue* 44 | **Everyone**: "Good-morning, Headmaster!"
Black-out | (Page 55) |

EFFECTS PLOT

ACT I

Cue 1   Darkness. When ready   (Page 1)
Children singing "Jesus Loves The Little Children"

Cue 2   **Hemsley**: " ... by the name of Albert Nuttall ... "   (Page 6)
Children sing "Vote ... for Albert Nuttall," distantly

Cue 3   **Tope**: " .. for such an honour."   (Page 7)
Handbell

Cue 4   **Albert**: " ... I can't read what they say, Miss ... "   (Page 14)
Bring up echo effect

Cue 5   **Albert**: " ... please, please see me!"   (Page 15)
Echo subsides and is gone

Cue 6   **Enid** and **Albert** hug each other   (Page 15)
Strange and haunting music

Cue 7   Black-out   (Page 15)
Sounds of a noisy playground

Cue 8   **Albert** is left winded and crying   (Page 19)
Music

Cue 9   Lights come up   (Page 19)
Music fades

Cue 10   Black-out   (Page 23)
Music

Cue 11   **Albert** joins **Enid**   (Page 24)
Music fades; train rushes past

Cue 12   Lights come up   (Page 24)
Another train rushes past

Cue 13   Lights grow dimmer   (Page 25)
Train rushes past

Cue 14   Black-out   (Page 26)
            Children's choir sings "Silent Night"

Cue 15   **Miss Partington**: "Oh, dear ... "   (Page 27)
            Handbell sounds loudly

Cue 16   **Miss Partington** walks away   (Page 28)
            Music: Christmas Carol; perhaps "Little Donkey"

Cue 17   **Shane**: " ... I can't act with animals."   (Page 29)
            Handbell sounds

ACT II

Cue 18   When ready   (Page 34)
            Music

Cue 19   **Miss Mint** walks into the bright pool of light DS   (Page 34)
            Music fades

Cue 20   Lights fade to black-out   (Page 36)
            Music creeps in

Cue 21   Lights on school hall fade   (Page 38)
            Music

Cue 22   Lights come up on headmaster's study   (Page 38)
            Music fades

Cue 23   Lights slowly fade to black-out   (Page 40)
            Music, birds, farmyard noises

Cue 24   **Albert**: "Who are you?"   (Page 43)
            Cue sounds are cut

Cue 25   Lights come up on **Albert**'s Home   (PAge 43)
            Train thunders past

Cue 26   **Eric**: " ... piggin' gypsies ... "   (Page 45)
            Train whistle blows

Cue 27   The lights fade to black-out   (Page 46)
            Music

Cue 28   **Albert** and **Miss Partington** embrace   (Page 46)
            Music fades

Cue 29   **Miss Partington** walks off. Silence   (Page 50)
            Music creeps in

Cue 30   Lights come up on **Albert**'s Home   (Page 50)
            Music fades; train whistle blows in the distance

Cue 31   **Albert** lies on the bed   (Page 50)
            Sound of breaking glass

Cue 32   Lights fade on **Albert**'s Home   (Page 51)
            Echo effect on **Primrose**'*s voice*

Cue 33   **Primrose** dances   (Page 55)
            Music; children singing "Vote ... for Albert Nuttall."

—